W9-AKC-840

Donated to
SAINT PAUL PUBLIC LIBRARY

COMING
APART

Also by Roger Rosenblatt

COMING APART

A Memoir of the Harvard Wars of 1969

ROGER ROSENBLATT

LITTLE, BROWN AND COMPANY

BOSTON   NEW YORK   TORONTO   LONDON

First Edition

The author is grateful for permission to include the following previously copy-
righted material: Excerpts from the minutes of the Faculty of Arts and Sciences
meetings reprinted by permission of the faculty members and Harvard University.

Library of Congress Cataloging-in-Publication Data

Rosenblatt, Roger.
    Coming apart : a memoir of the Harvard wars of 1969 /
Roger Rosenblatt. — 1st ed.
        p.   cm.
    Includes index.
    ISBN 0-316-75726-8
    1. Harvard University — Students — Political activity — History — 20th
century.   2. Student movements — Massachusetts — Cambridge —
History — 20th century.   3. Students for a Democratic Society (U.S.)
I. Title.
LD2160.R65   1997
378.1'98'1097444 — dc20   96-43051

10 9 8 7 6 5 4 3 2 1

MV-NY

Published simultaneously in Canada
by Little, Brown & Company (Canada) Limited

Printed in the United States of America

To John V. Kelleher, who
taught me and many others
what a university should be

ACKNOWLEDGMENTS

A GOOD MANY PEOPLE were of direct help in jogging or correcting my memory of events and otherwise in offering their thoughts and wise counsel. My thanks to them, most of whom are noted in the text. Among others to whom I would like to express deep appreciation are my agent, Gloria Loomis, for her friendship and guidance; Lee Aitken, for invaluable leads and references; Marios V. Broustas, for his thorough and thoughtful research assistance; and Jane Freeman, for her careful preparation of the manuscript and her characteristically astute comments on it. I am especially grateful to my editor, Jim Silberman. No writer could ask for a stronger ally, a sharper critic, or a more scrupulous second conscience.

COMING
APART

CHAPTER 1

ON APRIL 9, 1969, as the clanging of church bells was about to announce noon to Harvard Yard, I was standing in front of Sever Hall, surveying my world. Sever was located at the west end of the Tercentenary Quadrangle, called the New Yard to distinguish it from the older Yard next to it, in which some of the late-eighteenth- and early-nineteenth-century buildings — freshman dormitories named for New England worthies and benefactors like William F. Weld, Nathan Matthews, and Nathaniel Thayer — still stood. The two sections of the Yard were separated by University Hall, a long, four-story light-gray stone structure designed by Charles Bulfinch in 1815 that housed many of the University's administrative offices. A bronze John Harvard, a likeness of the first benefactor that the sculptor Daniel Chester French guessed at in 1882, posed in front of University Hall sitting in a chair on a pedestal. Sever Hall, which stood across from University Hall at the opposite end of the New Yard, was a dusky-purple Romanesque mon-strosity where most of the classes in literature were held, and where, just before noon on that day, I was about to teach mine, in modern poetry.

The New Yard was a patchy lawn, brown and pale green, cut into triangles and rhombuses by pathways. The ancient trees were still bare from the winter. One near-dead oak had a cemented knothole high on its trunk; its limbs twisted to-ward a clean blue sky. On the pathways, students and pro-fessors silently made their way toward their classes, some striding purposefully, some sleepwalking.

To my right stood Memorial Church, called Mem Church, the source of the bells, looking as confident and content as any Congregational church in any New Eng-land town. Above the church's gray-blue double door was a stone slab that read: "In grateful memory of the Harvard men who died in the World War, we have built this church."

To my left, directly across the Yard from the church, was the Harry Elkins Widener Memorial Library, known as Widener. The monumental library, built in 1913 and containing over three million books, was the center of Harvard scholarship. It was a gift in honor of Widener, a Philadelphia millionaire who died aboard the *Titanic*. On that unusually warm April morning, students sat reading on Widener's high stone steps. A young father carrying a baby on his shoulder and dragging a stroller descended the steps with care.

Depending on where one was standing, the Yard took on a different character. If one looked across from Widener at Mem Church, the place was a religious institution. If one looked over from the church to Widener, it became a repository of knowledge and tradition. The view of University Hall from Sever presented a government and business complex. Looking back over at Sever, one saw the house of classrooms, where learning was process. These four sides of the Yard were the four sides of Harvard — church, state, tradition, and discovery. On April 9, I was standing closest to discovery.

At the age of twenty-eight, I was in my first year of a two-year appointment as the Briggs-Copeland Instructor in English, which later became a five-year appointment as Briggs-Copeland Assistant Professor of English. The chair, which was not tenured, went to a junior faculty member who was expected to teach advanced courses in writing, in addition to regular literature courses. Among my students in English C, the writing seminars, were the novelist Mark Helprin, author of *Winter's Tale* and *Memoir from Antproof Case*, who became a speech writer for 1996 presidential candidate Bob Dole; and the *New York Times* drama critic and columnist Frank Rich.

I also held an administrative position, that of Allston-Burr Senior Tutor, or resident dean, in Dunster House. The Harvard Houses were dormitories for sophomores, juniors, and seniors. The older ones, great Georgian palaces, had massive wood-paneled dining halls and high, impressive towers. Dunster was the oldest, built in 1931. Its tower looked like an Arabian tent mounted on a white gazebo. The House sat on Memorial Drive, or Mem Drive, the thoroughfare that ran alongside the Charles River. In winters, the wind rode the cold in from the river and covered the House like a sheet over the dead.

My wife, Ginny, and I lived in the Senior Tutor's suite, a ground-level apartment, with our first child, Carl, who was nearly three. Ginny was pregnant with our daughter, Amy, who would be born on April 19. At Amy's birth the House staff lit up the Dunster tower — one of the few celebratory events in that momentous and shattering spring.

Of course, I had no intuition that anything momentous or shattering was about to happen as I waited in front of Sever for my class to begin. The sun shed its thickening light on Harvard Yard, and everything seemed to be bright and intact. Wearing my young professor's uniform of a Harris tweed jacket and charcoal gray slacks, my green book bag slung over my shoulder, I heard the bells toll and bounded up the Sever steps, two at a time.

"Still in love with the students?" asked Jere Whiting, who was coming down the steps as I went up. Professor Jeremiah Barrett Whiting, wall-eyed and dry as an old pump, had taught Chaucer at Harvard for decades.

"Crazy about 'em," I said and smiled, before setting him up. "It's their *electricity* when they really get hold of an idea."

"How do you know they don't have their wires crossed?" asked Whiting.

The poem I was about to teach was Wallace Stevens's "Anecdote of the Jar," which had puzzled me. It began:

> *I placed a jar in Tennessee,*
> *And round it was, upon a hill.*
> *It made the slovenly wilderness*
> *Surround that hill.*

What I had never worked out was: Did Stevens think that it was a good idea to place a jar in Tennessee? I had always looked at the poem from the air; that is, I was a giant hand, like God's, and I decided to place a jar in the state of Tennessee. A round jar lowered into a rectangular state. So what did that act accomplish? Did it civilize the slovenly wilderness or muck it up, being unslovenly and manmade? The jar certainly altered the nature of the wilderness, gave it a kind of order; one's attention was drawn to it. Did Stevens like it for that? Or did he prefer to see the wilderness untouched? What was the reader supposed to prefer? What was I to think?

The class went well. We talked of jars and Tennessee. We talked of the word *Tennessee*, how it looked long and narrow like the shape of the state. We talked of the word *jar*, how it also meant "to upset." We talked of the idea of being ajar, thus opening the wilderness. We talked of Stevens's further description of the jar, that "it was tall and of a port in air." We talked of what a port did, what a port was. We talked of the word *port* and of its etymology —

the French *porter*, "to carry." What did the jar carry? To what was it a port? And on and on, about words and wildernesses and the austere, lush, world-removed mind of Wallace Stevens.

When class was over, I walked out of the dark building and stopped and blinked. There on the opposite side of the Yard, hundreds of people were chanting and shouting. From the windows of University Hall, students leaned out and yelled to other students. The red and black banner of the radical Students for a Democratic Society (SDS) hung from a window on the second floor. Someone in a freshman dorm was playing the Beatles' song "Revolution" at enormous volume. A young man with half his body out the window above the SDS banner was making announcements through a bullhorn.

During the hour I was teaching, about three hundred students and others seized University Hall. Many were SDS members, some were followers, and a few were people from outside the University. After a brief rally held in front of the building, in which they presented a list of demands to the University, they marched up the stone steps and through the two green doors on each side of the building and swarmed into the offices of the administration. One of the occupiers played a tambourine.

SDS had started at Harvard when it had begun nationally, in 1962, but it did not become large or influential until the anti–Vietnam war march in Washington, D.C., in 1965. Another radical group, Progressive Labor (PL), was an offshoot of the Communist party and was both more violent than SDS and more straitlaced culturally; its members were pro-marriage, anti–drug taking, anti–rock 'n' roll, and short-haired. Both groups existed semi-comfortably under the SDS umbrella, but they were united when it came to opposing the war and the University's attachment to it — which was what this takeover of University Hall was about.

When the students came upon the deans working at their desks, they demanded that they leave or else they would be thrown out.

Fred Glimp, Dean of the College, stood in the office of Franklin Ford, Dean of the Faculty of Arts and Sciences, on the second floor. Both men were in their forties and looked more like businessmen than academicians. Both had gray, close-cropped hair; both were dressed in suits; and both were in manner and attitude "grown-ups." They could have passed for secret service agents — though Glimp was the most courteous and the friendliest of deans, and Ford was a first-class scholar of German history. In appearance they were in near-comic contrast to the student invaders, many of whom were shaggy-haired and dressed in jeans and t-shirts.

On leaving Ford's office, Glimp confronted one of the occupiers. "Get out of this building now," he told him.

"You don't have the authority to tell me anything," the student responded. Then he grabbed the arm of a University photographer who had come into the room and would not let go until the photographer had identified himself.

Glimp went downstairs and was barred by students from entering the reception area outside his office. He ordered those students to leave the building and was told that it was not up to him to give orders to anybody. He went back upstairs to the Faculty Room on the second floor, the south entrance to which had been blockaded with furniture.

Deans Glimp, Ford, and J. Peterson Elder, Dean of the Graduate School of Arts and Sciences, a jovial, old-boy classics scholar turned administrator, returned downstairs and told a group of about thirty students to leave. The students jeered at them. Ford asked the students: "Do you want to discuss this?"

"There's nothing to discuss," they told him.

Someone yelled at Glimp that he had "better get the hell out of here." A student pushed him toward the outside steps, but he went back into the hallway, where, near the south stairs, he saw two students holding another student while a third punched him. Glimp was then pushed out of the building.

Robert B. Watson, the Dean of Students, shouted at one of the occupiers: "You have no right to be in this building. I am ordering you to leave or face discipline."

The student responded: "We've taken this building; now get the fuck out of here."

Watson was a tall, wiry man in his late fifties who seemed more like a high school coach than a college dean. (In the fall he had enraged student radicals by referring to them as "sons of active Communists." He later apologized to a student-faculty committee for his "lapse of judgment.") He was pushed and dragged through the halls. According to his later testimony, a student grabbed him and tried to shove him down the south stairs but stopped when others said to leave him alone.

F. Skiddy von Stade, Dean of Freshmen, and Archie C. Epps, an Assistant Dean of Freshmen, were roughed up and hustled down the stairs. Epps was the only black man in the administration, and because of that he suffered the radical students' particular derision. He was pushed against a wall, then down a flight of stairs, then up against a water cooler, and out the northwest door. He reentered the building after having been thrown out and was thrown out again. That took some strenuous pushing and shoving, since Epps was very wide and built low to the ground like a football noseguard; had he been willing, he could have leveled two or three of his attackers with one shot. Assistant Deans William E. Russell and Burris Young were also driven out. Another assistant dean, James E. Thomas, a chatty Southerner, who was small and slight, was tossed over somebody's shoulder and carried from the building.

Accounts of how rough the occupiers were differed. Bill Russell, now a professor of education at Boston University, was one of a long line of Harvard Russells. He had black hair and strong features — handsome in the way of the young Fredric March — and he walked with a limp from childhood polio. He recalled that the occupiers were, on the whole, gentle.

"When the group of activists entered our office area," he said, "there was not a lot of loud commotion. Those whose 'job' it was to throw us out simply asserted that we must leave. I had purposefully retreated to my own little office, where I stood when I was approached by an activist, who told me in a firm but civil tone that I had to get out. I said I preferred to stay and tried to engage in discussion about the inappropriate and unjustified demands. I resisted enough to cause him to put his arm around my back as if to escort me, which is exactly what he had to do because I stopped every two or three steps to talk.

"Once out on the front steps, through a pretty tight crowd in the building by then, and to some cheering by those outside who supported the evictions, I made my way around to the back of the building beneath my office window, which was, by then, open. I saw on my office wall the large, framed copy of the portrait of my great-grandfather, William Eustus Russell, who had served two terms as governor of Massachusetts while he was in his thirties and was known as 'the boy governor.' I suddenly feared for the portrait's safety, so I yelled up to the activist who was in my office, explained that he was in my office, explained that the portrait had sentimental value, and asked if he would hand it down to me. He did, without much hesitation, as I recall. This was consistent with the kind of civil, sober, even respectful attitude on the part of the invaders, perhaps due to their sense of doing something wrong against individuals, some of whom they knew, others whom they knew of — a certain caution connected to conscience, and an understanding that, as individuals, we were really not the enemy."

Burris Young remembered the event as less polite. Like Russell, he was a popular dean with students and had lived in a freshman dorm for many years. Young was a throwback to the genteel Harvard of the 1950s — or the 1850s. Plump, kindly, bubbling with bonhomie, he used to serve friends stingers in his rooms at night. He was standing in Glimp's office when the occupiers broke into the building.

"We never thought they'd do it," he said. "One of the worst of them started to drag Skiddy [von Stade] down the hall. Skiddy had a bad back and he was in his sixties. I yelled out, 'Don't bend him over, you son of a bitch!'" Like many freshman proctors and deans, von Stade had the bearing and temperament of a friendly boarding school headmaster. He came from the horsey aristocracy of upstate New York, had leathery skin, and spoke with a loud, hail-fellow voice. It was said that he once had kept polo ponies at Harvard. He looked terrific in riding boots.

"It was really a terrible moment," Young told me. "I recognized one of my former students. He was in tears. I said to him, 'Jamie, Jamie. What are you doing?' He said, 'Burris, I *have* to.' He was weeping. Until then, we had never seen any rough stuff at Harvard. *You* remember," he told me. "We were so *innocent*."

Young was ejected with such force that he was prevented from falling to the ground only by a crowd at the foot of the steps.

In a sense, the ejectors and the ejectees cooperated with one another for opposite purposes. Because of recent threats by SDS, the administration had been expecting some sort of attack. Elsewhere throughout the country universities had been exploding on a regular basis. Columbia had its massive takeover and riots in the spring and summer of 1968. Starting in January 1969, there had been student strikes and protests at San Francisco State (January 6), Brandeis (January 8), San Fernando Valley State College (January 9), Swarthmore College (January 9), Berkeley (February 4), the University of Wisconsin (February 12), the City College of New York (February 13), Duke (February 13), Rutgers (February 24), and at least a dozen other places. Harvard knew that its turn would come.

"I remember a shared sense of urgency about doing something forceful and dramatic in opposing the war," Miles Rappaport told me. Rappaport (class of 1971), a member of SDS, is now the secretary of state of Connecticut.

At a faculty meeting some weeks earlier, law professor Archibald Cox, who had served on a commission to study the Columbia University riots of the spring of 1968, advised Harvard officials that the wisest course after a building takeover was "fast bust or no bust." At a small strategy session shortly before the incident, Cox had advised the deans that should an invasion of their offices occur, they should not fight but not go willingly, either. If they exited without any show of resistance, a takeover would seem to have been agreeably accepted.

Cox, who was in his sixties, was an imposing figure at Harvard, in the special way that old New England liberals could be imposing. He had a tall, rocklike bearing and that cold-water New England voice; his crew cut looked like iron filings; he had built a reputation for liberal right-thinking and fair-mindedness. He had served as solicitor general under President Kennedy, and in the 1970s he would serve as Attorney General Elliot Richardson's special prosecutor in the Nixon administration. In the "Saturday Night Massacre," which turned out better for the massacred than for those who had ordered it, Nixon demanded that Richardson fire Cox for seeking access to White House tape recordings. Richardson refused, and both men were fired.

Once the deans were expelled, the mob occupied both their offices and the elegant Faculty Room on the second floor. Until that spring, faculty meetings had been held in that room, originally a chapel. It was a large room with tall windows and a high ceiling from which chandeliers made of strings of crystal hung on long chains. The air was heavy with the smell of old wood, and the walls were crowded with oil portraits of former Harvard presidents. A photograph in *Life* magazine published the following week showed a distracted-looking long-haired student with his hand languidly resting on a white marble bust — a vivid representation of the assault on tradition by revolution. Until April 9, the room had been adequate for faculty meetings, because faculty meetings, being tedious, had always been poorly attended. After that afternoon, it was hard to find a place in the University large enough for everyone.

The occupiers, flush with victory, sat around on folding chairs and discussed tactics. Most of them were intense, some a little scared, some giddy. They voted not to smoke marijuana and not to damage the building, though a few people defaced the walls. On a wall in Glimp's office, someone had scrawled with a blue crayon, "Fuck authority." Others tried to obliterate the message unsuccessfully with white spray paint. There were shouting matches among contending factions. The Harvard radio station WHRB set up a studio in the building and began to broadcast. A Boston talk show interviewed one of the occupiers.

"Mainly the atmosphere was fun," Michael Kazin told me. Kazin was one of the three co-chairs of SDS. The son of the literary critic Alfred Kazin, he is now a professor of history at American University in Washington, D.C. "But it was more than an adolescent rebellion," he said. "We did not aim simply to desecrate the temple. We were fighting a war to stop a war."

Then the leaders made an announcement: "We are holding University Hall to force the Harvard Corporation [the University's highest governing body] to yield to our demands. We intend to stay until we win. These demands are nonnegotiable, and for very good reasons. For instance, we consider the ROTC as a life-and-death issue for the people of the world whose lands are occupied by U.S.

troops; whose social revolutions are fought viciously by the U.S. military."

Among their "Six Demands" to the five-member Corporation were to abolish Army, Navy, and Air Force officer training programs; to replace ROTC scholarships with regular scholarships; to refrain from tearing down Harvard-owned residences in slum neighborhoods to make way for new structures; and to roll back the rents. This last demand was part of a general effort of the SDS to ally themselves with blue-collar workers in Cambridge — an alliance that the workers scorned. But the main objective of the demands — as it was for all major political protests during those years — was to end the Vietnam war.

In fact, Harvard's record with ROTC was better, in terms of delimiting its power and position, than that of a great many universities. Three months before the University Hall takeover, the faculty had voted to deny credit for ROTC courses and had voted that ROTC officers should not be considered as members of the faculty. Even *The Nation*, which severely criticized Harvard that spring, conceded in an editorial on April 28 that Harvard had acted against ROTC "earlier than many and as soon as most."

The atmosphere in the Yard changed as I observed it from early afternoon to late. When I first stood outside University Hall, the crowd of students and professors showed a mixture of excited curiosity, playfulness (due mostly to the sunny weather), and the sort of guilty fascination of watching a fire. By about 2:30, when it was becoming clear that the occupiers were in the building to stay, the mood of the crowd grew quieter and more pensive. As the occupiers settled in — some of them posturing and making speeches on the steps and through the open windows — the crowd outside became annoyed. Several students started to taunt the occupiers in the building. Others set SDS leaflets on fire and raised a placard that read, "SDS Get Out." Many teachers were enraged when it was reported that people were rifling through confidential University files.

Al Gore, Vice President of the United States, who was a senior in Dunster House at the time, recalled "walking by University Hall during the occupation and feeling a swirl of emotions. I remember fringe statements on the left that held that violence was justified, but I don't know that many of us were swayed to the left. We had sympathy for the cause but not the tactics."

"This is a real tragedy," the freshman dean von Stade told a *New York Times* reporter, who described him as "shaking with anger." A sophomore, Thomas L. Saltonstall, of the distinguished Massachusetts family, remarked, "Student sentiment is in favor of getting ROTC off campus, but they do not believe in these tactics."

Michael Kazin said, "We were amazed that we didn't have more support, but we thought that support would build."

Some of the occupiers may have been ambivalent as well, or they may have just gone along for the ride. Alan

Heimert, a professor of English and Master of Eliot House, noted that an Eliot House sophomore who had joined in the takeover left University Hall by way of a window that afternoon to play in a House volleyball game. When the game was over, he returned to resume his attack on the University.

The faculty members standing around had widely divergent reactions. Some few wanted to join in the occupation. More, like myself, simply watched and wondered. Martin Peretz, the editor in chief of *The New Republic*, who was then an assistant professor of government and a well-known antiwar activist, had an intimation of the future. "I went over to University Hall to gawk," he recalled. "And I remember having a thought about civility. I was thinking that it would be very hard for any teacher, ever again, to get automatic and reflexive respect — the sort of respect you and I gave teachers. I thought this was a bad thing. I also think that the sight of the takeover was the beginning of my turn politically, from left to right."

Peretz wore a bushy beard in those days, which made him look like a cross between Moses and Karl Marx. To many adoring students he was both. "I still feel guilty about one of those kids," he says today, of the tearful occupier to whom Burris Young referred, "though I'm probably overestimating my influence on him. But he learned about leftist politics in my class, and then he went to extremes."

At about three o'clock, Glimp called a meeting of the Administrative Board, known as the Ad Board, which consisted of various undergraduate deans and administrators. As a Senior Tutor, I served on this board, the traditional function of which was to decide which students were to be placed on, or taken off, academic probation; whether students who had been dismissed for one or another reason should be reinstated; and similar, fairly tame, matters of discipline.

So pro forma was the work of the Ad Board that Edward T. (Ted) Wilcox, director of the program of general education and director of the freshman seminar program, toyed with the idea of inventing a game like Monopoly, called Administrative Board, in which the players sat around doing essentially nothing. Wilcox was a smart, funny, and boyish man who bounced around Cambridge on a motorcycle. His wife, Maud, was the great humanities editor at Harvard University Press. They had a cabin in Maine that lacked a toilet. Wilcox also thought up a collective noun for deans: a dither.

Little by little, the Ad Board had been getting increasingly involved with student protests over the past couple of years and had meted out mild punishments. Up to the University Hall incident, the student protests had been relatively restrained. Board members did not regard them casually but still felt that they could deal with them according to the established rules of civil behavior. The students, including many of the protesters, had grudgingly accepted the punishments — admonitions, rebukes, and, at the most severe, probation for a term. Meanwhile, the more violence-prone protesters had been growing restive because their antiwar activities had not been getting the attention they wanted.

The Ad Board meeting was brief but significant in terms of what was to follow in the next fourteen hours. Ted Wilcox remembered we discussed calling in the police — at least we discussed it obliquely. He believed the Ad Board knew that a "fast bust" was the choice of action. "We didn't say as much," he told me, "but you ought to have read it in the ellipses." Peter Wood, a widely admired graduate student in history and Senior Tutor in Eliot House, who is now a professor of history at Duke, recalled that we Senior Tutors were asked to look at photographs of the takeover, to identify students in our Houses. Whatever disciplinary purpose this might serve later, it made us all uncomfortable. Suddenly many of us did not recognize anybody.

My own memory is that no decision about taking an action was reached or even debated at length, but that may be because I arrived at the meeting late and did not participate in most of the discussion. What I did hear was that we were to go back to the Yard and try to keep the students outside the hall as calm as possible. Bill Russell heard what I heard. Referring to the night that followed, he said: "I was encouraged to get a few hours' sleep by Glimp and was persuaded, because things had become relatively calm, and because no one I consulted thought that anything imminent was going to happen anyway."

It was agreed that the Yard be sealed off to prevent outsiders from joining the melee. After the meeting, I returned to the crowd outside the Hall and talked quietly with the students I knew. Everyone was jumpy. As it turned out, the decision about whether to call in the police was not up to the Ad Board anyway.

At 4 P.M., Franklin Ford mounted the steps of Widener and pointed a bullhorn up at the second floor of University Hall. "In my capacity as Dean of the Faculty of Arts and Sciences," he said, "I should like to read a brief statement." Students at the bottom of the steps shouted, "Go away!" and "Shut up!" He announced that the Yard would be closed "until further notice." He warned the occupiers that they would be subject to criminal trespass charges if they did not get out of the building in fifteen minutes. A student yelled obscenities at him. About twenty students vacated at once; the rest remained. At 4:30 all but one of the entrances to the Yard were locked.

CHAPTER 2

THE UNIVERSITY HALL takeover was the culmination of a series of protests that had occurred at Harvard over the prior three years. The first came in the fall of 1966, when students erupted in a spontaneous demonstration against Secretary of Defense Robert McNamara, who was visiting the school to make a speech at Quincy House. When McNamara was finished, he climbed into his car, which was immediately engulfed by students shouting anti–Vietnam war slogans. They sat on the car. They rocked it back and forth. Eventually, they let it pass. There followed many expressions of woe and disapproval from the Harvard administration.

From that incident it became immediately apparent that there was an anxious fury among the students waiting to resurface. Yet it was also clear that the sizable majority of students did not approve of violent tactics. Within two days, 2,700 Harvard students had signed a letter of apology to McNamara.

After the McNamara incident, the protests became more frequent, more organized, and more desperate. Draft card burnings followed sit-ins followed rallies and more sit-ins. None of these activities was directed against the University. But, in the fall of 1968, a recruiter from the Dow Chemical Company, which (among more benign pursuits) manufactured napalm, was held "prisoner" for a few hours in a classroom in the Mallinckrodt Laboratory, a huge, high-pillared federal building where he was conducting interviews. This was a direct protest against University recruiting practices. A rule was passed by SFAC, the Student-Faculty Advisory Committee, which said that any company recruiting at Harvard would have to discuss its policies publicly if five hundred students petitioned it to do so. As a result, several institutions, such as the Georgetown University Medical School, refused to recruit at Harvard.

From the beginning of the academic year 1968–69, the level of student unhappiness, both with Harvard and with the war, had risen considerably. On September 22, an AWOL Marine, Paul Olimpieri, took refuge in the Divinity School Chapel. Divinity School students chained themselves to him. "We'd rather be wise and sensitive than clear," said the Divinity School dean, Krister Stendahl. Later, after he was arrested, Olimpieri accused the school of using him as a publicity gimmick.

On October 3, James D. Watson, a professor of chemistry who won the Nobel Prize as one of the discoverers of

DNA, was forced to admit that he had worked on a secret presidential panel that was looking into biological and chemical warfare. He claimed that he had quit the panel because "decisions we were being asked to make were primarily political, not scientific." This was one of several incidents that many students felt revealed the ties of the Harvard faculty and administration to the war effort. Another was the appointment of Henry Kissinger, professor of government, as Nixon's national security adviser.

On October 24, SDS accelerated its efforts against ROTC. Members said that they had collected three to four hundred signatures on a petition demanding the immediate ouster of ROTC. On November 19, SFAC voted down a resolution similar to the SDS petition. So highly charged was the political climate that fall, everyone seemed shocked at how elated the University could become when the Harvard football team tied mighty Yale on November 23. Since Harvard caught up to Yale by scoring sixteen points in the last minute and a half, the headline of the *Crimson*, the Harvard daily newspaper, read: "Harvard Beats Yale 29–29."

On December 11, the faculty agreed to discuss the ROTC question at Paine Hall, another federal-revival building outside the Yard, which housed the music department. SDS threatened a sit-in. Dean Glimp said that the faculty would cancel the meeting rather than attempt a showdown with student demonstrators. Glimp announced that a sit-in would be considered "a very serious offense."

But a hundred students did sit in and refused to leave. Glimp canceled the faculty meeting. There was much debate among the faculty as to how severely the demonstrators should be punished. Some thirty-five students were put on probation and their scholarships rescinded. This was to become an issue later. It was noteworthy, in terms of the subsequent hostility shown between faculty and administration, that the Ad Board originally had recommended that five students who were involved in both the Paine Hall and Dow demonstrations be expelled, but the faculty overturned the recommendation, giving the less severe punishment of probation to the demonstrators instead.

On February 3, a faculty-sponsored meeting was held to discuss the role of the military at Harvard. Over seven hundred students attended. Shortly afterward the faculty voted to take away Corporation appointments from ROTC faculty and to strip ROTC of academic credit.

Between that date and early April, no mass demonstrations were held. But Harvard, which throughout the fall term was debating other urgent issues — whether Radcliffe should retain its separate identity or be absorbed into Harvard; the establishment of an Afro-American studies major, or as Harvard called it, a concentration; and the total revision of several departments — was in a brittle and agitated state.

On March 6, a former Columbia University graduate student named King Collins burst in on a social relations class in the company of several followers. A few days later, Collins and his cohorts — none of them Harvard students — invaded Eliot House. They took off all their clothes and tossed them in washing machines in the laundry room. A confrontation between naked protesters and suited deans followed, which, because of the tense atmosphere, was not as hilarious as it ought to have been.

Over the next week, Collins led other classroom disruptions and was eventually arrested for assault and battery. There was a brief demonstration of about a hundred SDS students that broke up an SFAC meeting with University president Nathan Marsh Pusey on ROTC. On the evening of April 8, there was a huge SDS rally during which a more serious act of protest was promised by the SDS leaders.

University Hall was it. Looking at the students leaning out the windows of University Hall, hearing the defiant, exuberant shouting, and watching the other students who were observing them with apprehension, dread, and pleasure, one had no doubt that the protests had hit a new and, to the University, much more threatening level.

"On the surface it seems ironic that the University should be under attack because socially concerned students have a quarrel with society," Archie Cox observed in a speech shortly after the takeover. "Part of the answer is that often when one is angry, he kicks the nearest shin. If you prefer psychological terms, the University becomes the surrogate for society, upon which the student can vent his frustration. As one boy put it, 'We know our quarrel is with Washington, but we can't reach Washington; we do know how to hurt the University administration.'"

Al Gore told me: "I always thought that there was something off concerning the students' choice of target. I guess, if the University was the most convenient, then that was the target you chose."

Oddly, I was involved, to a greater or lesser degree, in all the demonstrations that led up to University Hall. I say oddly because I cannot imagine anyone with less knowledge, much less passion, about Vietnam, Harvard investments, University-owned property, or most of the other issues that the students protested, which were to become codified in the list of demands made by the occupiers of University Hall. This was the raging 1960s, but I felt no rage about anything, except civil rights. Like most everyone at Harvard, I opposed the war, but that was it. I rarely read a newspaper or watched TV news. When I wasn't studying or teaching, I was playing touch football, tennis, or basketball with friends and taking long family weekend drives into Vermont and New Hampshire.

The first connection I had with a political demonstration was a pure and crazy coincidence. It happened that one of the students involved in the blocking of McNamara's car was a freshman named Roger Rosenblatt. The two of us never met. I first learned of his existence when friends of his from Princeton wrote saying that they were coming up to spend a weekend with me, and when my namesake's rabbi wrote me an excoriating note about my failure to meet "my" Sunday School classes. It was more eerie than funny having a doppelgänger in the same university, especially when we bore an unusual name. Since the other Roger was far more involved than I in world affairs, I began to think of him as a scold.

After the McNamara incident, there was much handwringing about the limits of dissent, and a letter arguing that such demonstrations were the only right thing to do in the face of an evil war was sent to the editor of the *New York Times*. One of the signatories was Roger Rosenblatt. As soon as the letter was published, I began receiving phone calls and letters from friends and acquaintances congratulating me on the moral strength of my stand. I explained that the one they were extolling was another Roger Rosenblatt but always added that I admired his courage, too. In truth, I couldn't have cared less. But I do recall enjoying the feeling of being in the public eye on the right side of an issue, even if I had arrived there by proxy.

I was also a little afraid that the senior members of the English department would not like the idea of a revolutionary in their midst. But, to the contrary, it turned out that they, too, enjoyed the idea of morality by association, and while none of them ever mentioned the *Times* letter to me directly, it was evident that my stature (I was a fourth-year graduate student) had been elevated in their eyes. It was then that I learned that nothing was more important at Harvard than the mutual reassurance that everybody shared the same liberal beliefs about everything, even if that were not the case, and as long as those opinions did not put the believers in any real jeopardy.

The day of the takeover there had been one other demonstration. Shortly before dawn on April 9, some five hundred SDS members and antiwar protesters marched on the home of President Pusey. The president's house, which today is located on Elmwood Avenue, at a distance from the Yard, was then at 17 Quincy Street, a large, ivy-covered federal-style mansion about a hundred yards behind Sever Hall. They chanted, "Smash ROTC" and "ROTC must go." They stuck their list of demands to Pusey's door with a knife. Then they marched away toward the river, still chanting. When the demonstrators proceeded to march behind Lowell House, their opponents poured buckets of water from a third-story window and shouted, "Fuck you!"

Pusey was a figure of mixed reputation. To the majority of alumni, he was a bulwark of Harvard tradition, a hero who had opposed Joseph McCarthy in the 1950s (both at Harvard and before that, at Lawrence College in Appleton, Wisconsin, where he had taught classics) and who had also raised millions for the University. To the majority of the liberal faculty, he was a patrician pighead, not unlike Joseph Conrad's Captain McWhirr in *Typhoon*, who plowed ahead for the sake of plowing ahead. That his dignified physical appearance had not changed a whit over decades seemed to many a reflection of his mind.

If the "establishment" physical appearances of Ford and Glimp worked against them, Pusey's did so in spades. It was not simply that he had that "grown-up" bearing. His face was an institution itself — handsome, monumental, and implacable. He was, "when you got to know him," warm and thoughtful, or so I always found him on those few occasions when we talked together. He was devoted to Harvard, to scholarship, and to high standards of moral conduct. Occasionally he even showed a sly and quiet sense of fun. But he was not about to let people get close to him. Even his good looks were not as appealing as they should have been, because of the distance at which he held himself. The features of his face were near-perfectly formed, but their total composition looked like a police artist's sketch of a good-looking man.

Peretz observed that in a perverse way Pusey's unswerving rectitude may have provided a spur to the students' activism: "The smug sense of order in Nate Pusey's placid face may have encouraged the kids to think that chaos was more fun."

Michael Kazin confirmed that Pusey's appeal as an opponent "was that he was unlikely to bend. Liberals were the enemy. He was a liberal." Though he did not know it, his remark was a wry comment on the liberal faculty's dislike of Pusey.

Even Pusey's stalwart opposition to Joseph McCarthy was thought to be tainted by his attitude of moral superiority. Author and journalist J. Anthony Lukas recalled that in November 1953, when he was a reporter on the *Crimson*, he attended the first press conference Pusey held since becoming president. Senator McCarthy had accused physics professor Wendell H. Furry and other faculty members of Communist activities. Pusey said that McCarthy's comments on testimonies that were still secret were "against all the principles of our country." He would not condescend to discuss any action that Harvard would take against Furry. In an article for the *New York Times Magazine* in that spring of 1969, Lukas wrote: "This was the characteristic Pusey stance on McCarthy — irritated, moralistic, almost contemptuous. One often felt that the president could hardly bring himself to discuss the fulminations of the swarthy, uncouth Populist. . . . He warned that 'it would be a sorry thing if, in resisting totalitarianism, we were to follow the counsels of the frightened and adopt its methods.' But, most of the time, in the best Brahmin tradition, he tried to keep himself and Harvard above the fray."

To students, Pusey was at best remote, at worst prudish and narrow-minded. A devout Christian, he had once declared that Memorial Church was meant for Christian worship exclusively. In the 1950s, the University Preacher refused permission for a Jewish student to be married in the church. Pusey supported the decision. He said that Mem Church, though nondenominational, had always been thought of as a "Christian house of worship" and that anyone of another "religious persuasion" could find his own church. The faculty denounced him, and the

Corporation voted to allow students to be married in Mem Church with whatever service they chose.

Pusey made no effort to endear himself to the student radicals either. In his President's Report for 1966–67, he referred to "our self-professed student revolutionaries" as "Walter Mittys of the left." He also had always made clear that while he grudgingly accepted the faculty decision to downgrade ROTC, he personally was against it.

At 8 P.M. on April 9, as the Yard began to grow cold in the dark, he issued a statement on the takeover. "Can anyone believe the Harvard SDS demands are made seriously?" he asked. He referred to the faculty votes on ROTC and implied by his question that SDS was more interested in doing harm to Harvard than to the military.

By then, I was back at Dunster House. I told Ginny what had happened during the day, and we went to eat with the students in the House dining room. Everyone was quiet and nervous. Dunster House was known for its student activists (every Harvard House developed a reputation for a certain social or intellectual character, which changed every few years), but even here the majority of students were sour on the takeover, and had little sympathy for the SDS, except for sharing an opposition to — and a great fear of being drafted for — Vietnam.

"So what do you think?" I asked the students at our table.

"I think they're assholes," one responded. The others remained silent, brooding and staring into their food.

Meanwhile, the students in University Hall had called for a massive rally of undergraduates in their support. Gaining entry to the locked Yard was fairly easy, yet very few students showed up. Had nothing else occurred in the following hours, most student and faculty opinion would have swung strongly against the occupiers.

CHAPTER 3

B
UT A FEW MINUTES before 5 A.M. on April 10, three buses rolled into Harvard Square. Seconds later, four hundred state and local policemen from Cambridge, Somerville, Belmont, and Boston, wearing bright blue riot helmets with Plexiglas visors and carrying clubs and shields, swarmed into Harvard Yard. They lined up outside University Hall and waited as Dean Glimp called to the occupiers through a megaphone, "You have five minutes to vacate the building." The occupiers linked arms. Their leaders passed out small squares of cloth soaked in water, which they were to put over their mouths and noses to protect them from tear gas.

Jody Adams, a student in the Hall, reported in the *Crimson:* "I had no doubt that this was it. I found the six people there that I knew the best and attached myself to them. We had been told to stand in line and link our arms together, to form a solid mass of bodies that would represent the peaceful resistance — the only resistance — we were going to offer the cops. All of the people from up-stairs were waking up and gathering with us in the Hall. They were groggy and had puffy, sleep-swollen faces.

"When we were all there, the same loud voice told us that the gates had been opened, there were several patrol cars and paddy wagons driving up, and the cops were massing in the firehouse. I felt a dull sensation in my stomach at the sound of 'paddy wagons,' but I was really not afraid then. I was too sure that nothing bad could hap-pen. It would obviously be incredibly stupid for Harvard to pull anything really dirty at that point — it took so little sensitivity or intelligence to see that. I never really consid-ered the possibility of violence."

At this point, Michael Kazin decided to go out of Uni-versity Hall and scout around. "At the time I told myself that I was acting as a lookout," he said, "but maybe I left because I was scared too. As soon as I got to the steps of Widener, the police flooded the Yard. I ran back to the kids who were on the University Hall steps. Then I did some-thing foolish and threw an empty Coke bottle at the on-rushing cops. I got a billy club across my head. I bled a lot."

The mass of police rushed up the steps of University Hall. Students who were standing on the steps fled. The policemen, many of whom removed their badges, pursued them with nightsticks. They kicked the students, threw them to the ground, and beat them.

James Atlas, the Delmore Schwartz biographer who is now an editor at the *New York Times Magazine*, was a sophomore at the time and had been sitting all night on the University Hall steps in front of the door closest to Widener. Many students did this to show that they shared at least the antiwar sentiments of those in the building. Occasionally he went into the Thayer common room, a general meeting place for students in the nearby freshman dormitory, for coffee, and then returned to the steps.

"There was no real warning about the police," he recalled, "but there were rumors that they were massed near Pusey's house. I was sitting on the steps when they charged the Yard. First there was a burst of spotlights. They were flooding the Yard with light, to know where to shoot the tear gas. Once the Yard was lit up, they shot the tear gas out of canisters. The Yard was still dark, but a curtain of smoke hung over it. Then they came at the building, a phalanx. It was like a military operation. They wasted no time. It was pretty brutal."

Anna Fels, a New York physician and a writer, who is now married to Atlas, was also standing on the Hall steps. "Once I saw the police massing in the Yard," she said, "I knew that this was going to be a physically frightening, deadly event. This was no kids' game. They were playing for keeps. It was so far outside our experience. This wasn't Columbia, or New York. This was bucolic, intellectual Cambridge."

Jamie Gorelick, then a sophomore, who became deputy attorney general of the United States in the Clinton administration, was on the University Hall steps as well. She, too, was gassed and collapsed in a friend's room. "I expected some leadership from the University," she said. "I was caught between a respect for authority, despair at the war, and Harvard's seeming indifference."

Carol Sternhill, who teaches journalism at N.Y.U., was covering the takeover as a sophomore for the *Crimson*. She remembered, "There were tons of police in baby-blue helmets. I was standing on the steps nearest the chapel when they came at us. The demonstrators' arms were linked, and the police charged.

"Up to then, it had all been pretend. Then the police just grabbed people off the top steps and threw them down. People were screaming. It was a madhouse. I saw them beat up a guy in a wheelchair. I was so terrified. I ran and kept running. The whole thing was a shock to me. I don't think that I had ever seen anybody hit anybody before."

Michael Kinsley, the editor and writer, who was a freshman at the time, had a less emotional view of events. He was near the steps when the police charged. "I felt that the stories of police violence were exaggerated," he said. "I remember that kid in the wheelchair. And I remember thinking: Why did they put him in front of the steps, or why did he put himself there, if he did not expect to be hit? If they did not want the kid in the wheelchair to be in danger, then take him away from the steps. You can't have it both ways."

The doors to University Hall cleared, the police charged the building. They broke down the first doors with a three-foot battering ram. They clubbed the occupiers inside and dragged many of them out by their hair. About twenty students came out of the building with their heads bloodied. Others were injured as they jumped out the first-floor window to escape. Among those who jumped and avoided arrest were Joseph Seamans, a junior, whose father had been named secretary of the air force a few months earlier; and Arthur Schlesinger, son of historian Arthur Schlesinger Jr.

Afterward a student with his arm in a sling told a reporter: "Ten to fifteen state troopers rushed in and started clubbing the people immediately in front of me over the head. Then I was sprayed with Mace. I got this on my arm from trying to stop a cop from beating a girl who had two gashes in her head."

Jody Adams said: "The cops turned from the kids on the landing to us in the hallway. They started to push us back down the narrowing hallway to the dead end of the locked door at the other entrance. They charged the crowd swinging their clubs at the heads and middles of the kids up front. We fell back onto each other, but our arms were still linked tight. They kept beating at us, moving deeply into the crowd. I fell back on a black wooden Harvard chair, and about twenty people fell on top of me."

Some students who had been watching the bust ran from the Yard and were chased by police. William Alfred, professor of English and the author of the play *Hogan's Goat*, said that some of the police pursued people into the dorms. "Three or four boys were so terrified, they came over to my house and slept on the floor." Alfred had a Victorian house on Athens Street, about a block from Dunster House.

"I went out to see what was happening in the street," he said. "When I came back, one of the boys, who was nineteen years old, was asleep on the floor with his thumb in his mouth."

In all, forty-one students were reported injured, most of them suffering cuts to the head. Reporters covering the scene were also roughed up, including a reporter on the *Washington Post* and one from *Life* magazine, who was clubbed from behind and pummeled. A three-inch gash was bleeding over his right eye. At least seven policemen were treated for injuries as well. Contrary to what Adams and others said about the nonviolent nature of the resistance, police reported being hit by the heavy brass doorknobs that had been pulled off the doors and hurled at them.

The bust was over in minutes. Many students, including Miles Rappaport, were carted off to Cambridge City Jail, charged with trespassing. Rappaport told me that he was scared that night in jail. All were released the following morning.

News of what had happened spread down to the House at once. At Dunster, everyone was awakened by the House fire alarm, which someone had set off. I shot out of bed. Kids were yelling, "Bust!" With Ginny trying to calm our three-year-old, Carl, who was screaming from fright, I hauled on some clothes and ran up to the Yard. I could not have arrived more than fifteen minutes after the police had taken away the students. It was now about 5:45. Policemen remained in front of University Hall. They stood in a line, their legs planted apart, each holding a riot stick in front of his chest. Their faces were concealed by the Plexiglas visors attached to their helmets, which reflected the half-risen sun. They wore calf-high boots, jodhpurs with wide stripes down the side, and jackets that strained at the buttons.

Suddenly hundreds of students poured into the Yard. They taunted the police with cries of "Sieg Heil!" The police remained standing in an adamant wall. Finally they dispersed, to more cries and jeers. By the time the last of them had left, at around 6 A.M., the crowd had grown to nearly a thousand. They gathered on and around the steps of Widener as speakers exploded with anger at the University, and in particular at Pusey.

All morning this went on. Speeches were given in every corner of the Yard by SDS leaders, faculty members, anyone who had something to say, which seemed to be everyone. Clusters of students gathered around each speaker and cheered whenever Pusey and the administration were assailed. The actions of the police had swung opinions in favor of the occupiers, who in the folklore of the moment had become martyrs.

In the afternoon, moderate students who originally had been hostile to the University Hall takeover called a mass meeting in mammoth Memorial Hall to decry the bust. Located outside the Yard, across Cambridge Street, Mem Hall was a half-beautiful, half-terrifying Gothic structure, with its multicolored tower that was cut in two in the 1950s by a fire, causing the destruction of a giant clock. If Queen Victoria had been a building, Mem Hall would have been it. In its womb was Sanders Theatre, a gorgeous auditorium made of varnished wood, where the seats curved to embrace the stage and voices reverberated like cellos. This was where the students met.

About 1,500 students showed up and unanimously voted for a three-day boycott of classes. Some junior faculty members known for antiwar activities agreed to the boycott, which they called a strike. Some decided to hold their classes outside, on the grass — a compromise, they felt, between believing in teaching and believing in the students. Several resolutions were passed at the Memorial Hall meeting. One demanded that the "police not be brought onto the campus again." Another called for "immediate steps" to reconstruct the University government, so as to "include members of its entire University community." Another called for the resignation of Pusey. At the Law School, some five hundred students gathered and also voted for Pusey's resignation.

Martin Kaplan, who wrote the screenplay for *The Honorable Gentleman*, which starred Eddie Murphy, and who was then a Dunster House junior, said that before the bust, he had not only been opposed to the takeover, he had been generally apolitical. "After what Pusey did, however, I never felt the same way about Harvard. The betrayal effected my radicalization. I came from a typically Jewish middle-class home in New Jersey. Nothing had been more important to me than to go to Harvard. I had expected it to be the paragon of reason and conciliation and community. And then to be so let down by it."

David Hollander, who became president of the *Crimson* two years later and is now a New York lawyer, told me: "I still bear a grudge against Harvard for the bust."

Jamie Gorelick recalled: "I never really believed the rhetoric about Harvard being the all-powerful cog in the military-industrial complex. I was more concerned with its indifference. I felt the University should be an enlightened place."

As for the faculty, most of the immediate reaction was shock and dismay. Stanley Hoffmann, a professor of government, who until that time was a great favorite with left-leaning students, and who writes on European politics and U.S. foreign policy for publications like the *New York Review of Books*, recalled that Pusey's decision "was stupid. It was just plain stupid. But the man was stupid. And arrogant. Arrogant beyond belief."

Professor of economics John Kenneth Galbraith said: "The taking over of University Hall is not something I or most of the faculty would have endorsed. On the other hand, calling in the police was a terrible mistake."

My mentor, John V. Kelleher, professor of Irish history and literature, took Pusey's side, as did many of those who would later constitute the Conservative Caucus of the faculty, though he had his characteristically humane reservations.

"I remember the faculty meeting after the University Hall bust," he wrote to me, recalling events many years later. "We were treated to the full works by the orators, and the worst was an almost tearful address by a member of the philosophy department who begged us to consider the fact of police brutality. 'Think of it as one of your own children who had been beaten like that!' For the first and only time I wanted to get up and speak. I wanted to say that if it was one of my children, I could hardly wait to get him home so that I could give him a rousing kick where it wouldn't blind him. But I didn't, because an old friend was sitting in front of me; and his son had been in the Hall."

Nathan Glazer, professor of sociology and co-author of *Beyond the Melting Pot* with Daniel Patrick Moynihan, then professor of education and now a U.S. senator from New York, offered a dispassionate and prescient analysis at the time: "On every campus you get a few hundred who think that the university is a symbol of a corrupt, imperialistic society. But there is the question of police actions. It may force moderates to support the strike."

In general, the older Harvard alumni sided with Pusey against the students. "It's time somebody took a stand, and Pusey did," said a member of the class of 1926. "These people move heaven and earth to get into Harvard, and then they bite the hand that feeds them."

One alumnus referred to those fomenting the disruptions as "a hard core of commies." Ephron Catlin Jr., senior vice president of the First National Bank of Boston, told the *New York Times*: "The entry of the Students for a Democratic Society was an illegal act of civil disorder and had to be dealt with summarily. It is as if a gang walked into the First National Bank. We'd call in the police in a hurry." A member of a Boston investment house commented: "I don't think Harvard moved fast enough. I don't give a damn whose head got bloodied. If you get mixed up in a thing like that, you deserve what you get."

With all the finger-pointing and recriminations about who was responsible for the bust that ensued over the following weeks, Pusey held that the decision was his alone. He reiterated that to me recently, maintaining the view that his decision was the right one.

Yet, whether or not he realized it, what Pusey did by calling in the police was to unleash at least two centuries of town-gown hatred. Many of the cops who busted University Hall were the sons, nephews, cousins, and grandsons of all those Irish immigrants who had sailed to New England in the 1850s and afterward, only to come upon doors (often at Harvard) that read "NINA" — No Irish

Need Apply. They had been treated like the servants they, in fact, were by generations of rich Harvard boys who lived on the Gold Coast, the luxurious nineteenth-century residences south of the Yard that were built by America's wealthy for their sons. The boys called all the servants Biddie and Mack and passed them in the street as if they were walking through them. At last the uniformed and club-wielding descendants of these folks were offered the opportunity to, indeed were invited to, bash in a few of those snotty heads. The students in and out of University Hall, and most of the faculty, could not believe the rage revealed in the history lesson before our eyes.

Even if history was not haunting their minds, there was always the cops' resentment of the fact that students as privileged and cosseted as Harvard's should act as they did. The students — often seen as arrogant and unlovable — might rail against Vietnam, but there was scant danger of their going there. They were protected, as the sons and nephews of the cops were not.

The bust was class warfare in its rawest form. Henry Rosovsky, a professor of economics who later became Dean of the Faculty, said that he felt that the class hatred between Harvard and the rest of Cambridge "had always been kept under wraps until the bust." Galbraith said: "These kids were the favored members of the community. The Vietnam war was for poor conscripts — like the families of those police." Michael Walzer, the author of *Just and Unjust Wars*, now at Princeton's Institute of Advanced

Study, traced the class warfare to attitudes about the Vietnam war.

"I have fairly vivid memories of wandering through Harvard Yard a day after the bust," he said. "Talking to student friends who had been in the building about why they were in the building and what it was like, I remember a conversation with political philosopher Alastair MacIntyre, sometime that year, in which he described a police encounter with a student as an example of class struggle: the police represented the working class, and he, he said, was entirely on their side. I think that a very large number of working Americans saw it, at the time, the way he did. The cultural split on the left began then, the Harvard events being only a very marginal cause; we somehow escaped the kind of media attention that was focused on Berkeley and Columbia. I already had a fairly clear sense of what was coming, not because of any particularly acute perceptiveness but because of my experience with the Cambridge referendum on the war the previous fall. A graduate student in sociology did an analysis of the result and found that people were more likely to vote against the war the higher the rent they paid, the greater the value of their homes: it was the WASPs and Jews and the students of Harvard Square against East and North Cambridge. An awful situation, which any sort of student noise or stridency could only exacerbate."

Mike Kinsley said that "there really was a lot of false martyrdom" among the students. "Everybody felt guilty for our sense of privilege, and there we were in our cocoons at Harvard."

John Kelleher saw the student protesters as spoiled brats with an underdeveloped sense of history and a flair for self-protection. He recalled a demonstration after the bust, which he witnessed from his office at the rear of Widener.

"I remember hearing confused chanting and looking out my office window as a herd of marching students came down the steps from Lamont [library] and passed the back of Widener," he says. "They were led by girls and boys whose faces were aglow, some I think were dewy-eyed, with the spirit of solidarity in a righteous cause; and they were rhythmically chanting some slogans I couldn't make out. I could only think: A goddamn flock of sheep! And so they passed out of sight and earshot. But you can be sure of one thing: they stayed within the limits of the Yard."

At the Memorial Hall gathering, the "Six Demands" became eight. They eventually would become twelve. "Strike!" came the printed cry from the *Old Mole*, a radical sheet produced that spring to be the quasi-official voice of the students' rebellion. (The "old mole" was a metaphor taken from Karl Marx for those who relentlessly worked to overthrow the system.) "Strike for the Eight Demands," read the headline. The eight still included abolishing ROTC and rolling back Cambridge rents but now added absolving students who had been in University Hall from punishment, absolving those who had been put on probation in such previous demonstrations as Paine Hall, and creating a full-fledged department of black studies. Up until then, the faculty had decided to make black studies a "committee" rather than a department, which meant that it would be composed of faculty members from several departments and have a flexible structure. The difference between a department and a committee was important in terms of the stature and permanence of the subject, thus the issue was politically volatile. It would come to a head in a few weeks.

The "Strike!" poster created by the *Old Mole* was interesting for the disparate variety of its concerns: "Strike for the eight demands. Strike because you hate cops. Strike because your roommate was clubbed. Strike to stop expansion [of Harvard-owned rental properties]. Strike to seize control of your life. Strike to become more human. Strike to return Paine Hall scholarships. Strike because there's no poetry in your lectures. Strike because classes are a bore. Strike for power. Strike to smash the corporation. Strike to make yourself free. Strike to abolish ROTC. Strike because they are trying to squeeze the life out of you."

The mixture of complaints seemed random and illogically related. Vietnam was connected to the quality of life, which was connected to teaching and bloodshed and power. Yet for the students there was a definite relationship among these things. Their complaints had an odd kind of unity, in part because they were convinced that there was a unity, read conspiracy, in much of the America they opposed. At Harvard, and in the country for which it believed it stood, nothing was working — not the army, not the classes, not the cops, not the soul, not poetry or the teaching of poetry. For myself, I wondered what a teacher of poetry was supposed to be in a situation like that: the jar that gives order to Tennessee or part of the "slovenly" (read also free and imaginative) wilderness. I chose to be the jar.

CHAPTER 4

THE ATMOSPHERE of the days following the University Hall bust was like that after a thoroughgoing burglary of one's home. Fury mingled with a general helplessness — not only among the SDS members, who thrived on such feelings, but among the students at large, who felt isolated and confused. The students in Dunster House stayed up night after night, all night, holding mass meetings in the dining hall, yelling their hatred of the University, hollow-eyed, bewildered as to what action to take, not wanting to stay at the University, not wanting to go home and deal with their parents, debating whether SDS was for them, fearing that things were going too far but not knowing where they ought to go. They fought with their parents over the phone. Jim Atlas remembered having a huge fight with his folks. There was talk and more talk. Voices grew raspy, everyone dead tired.

As Senior Tutor it was my duty to stay up all those nights with the students; and, odd to say, it became my pleasure, too. I had nothing I wanted to do more. Like them I was often uninterested in my classes, in spite of what I had said to Jere Whiting about the "electricity" of teaching. I too wanted my life to feel more human. If I lacked the students' fire about Vietnam, I resented the war for what it was doing to the young people around me. Here, in this unlikely, small universe, I became a leader. I discovered that I had the gift of gab; I was a good ex tempore speech maker; I could be wryly funny and thus make it seem that irony was controlling passion — the ideal college humorist. And by using humor, of course, I could disguise my feelings about issues, which were as confused as anybody's.

I did believe in keeping the University intact; this was derived more from a traditional faith in the usefulness of long-lasting institutions than from anything personal. Most of my fellow junior faculty members shared this attitude. Yet, many of the senior faculty, who also believed in institutions, behaved as if they did not. This was oddly suicidal for a group that could earn its keep nowhere else in the world. At one of the noisier faculty meetings following April 9, Morton White, a professor of philosophy who later left Harvard for Princeton's Institute of Advanced Study, stood in the center of the room and, in a shrill voice, called Franklin Ford a "liar" for having reported a takeover of the third floor of Emerson Hall, the philosophy building. Ford's report was accurate, but White called him a liar in front of his colleagues anyway. "Mr. Dean, you are a liar." There were many such ugly moments at faculty meetings that spring and in the years to come. But at that particular moment, I began to realize that I wanted no part of University life, at least not then, and in my heart I began my slow, evolving exit.

Unlike many of the senior faculty, the junior faculty generally fought for the unity and coherence of Harvard. Doris Kearns (now Doris Kearns Goodwin), who has written biographies of Lyndon Johnson and Eleanor Roosevelt, was a resident tutor in government on the Dunster House staff. Tutors were advanced graduate students who guided undergraduates in their Honors work. She and other tutors and instructors stood beside me talking to the students in the Dunster dining hall in what seemed like endless town meetings on every one of those frantic, exhausting nights. Elsewhere in the University, other junior faculty members also rose to the occasion. Peretz stayed by his students, as did historian John Womack, the biographer of Zapata; the biologist-essayist Stephen Jay Gould; Edward Keenan, the Russian scholar; and James Thomson, a China scholar who had resigned from the Johnson White House staff over Vietnam and had won national attention for writing a blistering article in *The Atlantic* condemning the war.

Everyone's emotions were frazzled. Peretz recalled coming upon a group of students who were in his freshman seminar: "They had not been in University Hall, but many of them were in tears. All were very frightened.

They just wanted to talk." Students filled Bill Alfred's house on Athens Street and raged and wept.

A student in my modern poetry class stopped me after class to ask if she could speak to me. She was made pregnant by a married teacher, she said, and she was going to England to get an abortion. "I'm frightened," she told me. "I just wanted someone to know."

"Let me hear that you're okay when it's over," I said helplessly. She nodded and walked away toward Widener.

Years later she wrote me that she had made up the entire story. She had been so shaken by the events, she had worked herself into an irrational state and wanted to vent her emotions. "You were closer to my age," she explained. "I think I needed a reason to be hysterical."

Most of the senior faculty simply went home to dinner, letting their juniors hold up their institution for them. We were, after all, young, strong, and expendable. We could clean up the mess, hold the University together, run out our terms of appointment, and leave our elders a spotless, unthreatening house. Our absence would not matter to them. To us their absence really did not matter either. We had our own journey to undertake and understand — being caught, by age and position, in the middle.

We were a few years older than the students and more than a few years younger than the senior faculty. We had been too young for Korea and too old for Vietnam. We had grown up with the values of the 1950s, which were far less staid than they generally have been rendered, and with as much rebellion as conformity. We questioned institutions but we also fundamentally believed in them. We were outsiders to the institution we were defending, just as the students were outsiders to the institution they were attacking. Yet we believed in its worth. Unlike the baby boomers, we were few in number. We were uncelebrated and unselfconscious. We were our own distraught world.

Daily faculty meetings continued for the week following the bust — attended by as many as five hundred (over twice the usual number) in the Loeb Drama Center, the theater being one of the few places in the University large enough to accommodate everybody. Like the meetings of the students in the Houses, these were overlong, strained, and contentious. It was instructive for us junior faculty members to see our elders spew their anger at the administration — sometimes for old, obscure offenses that had nothing to do with University Hall. A professor who had been denied a raise ten years earlier, or a department chairman who had been thwarted in one way or another — this was their chance for revenge. At one point, even the unflappable Pusey barked (in his gentlemanly way) at Galbraith, an old enemy. Galbraith had made a speech critical of him. Pusey remarked: "I'm sure it gives you great pleasure to say that." Galbraith retorted: "I assure you, Mr. President, it does not."

At the meeting of April 11, Dean Ford defended Pusey's calling in of the police in the strongest terms: "For some people these past few days seem to have been very interesting," he told the faculty, "even exciting. Indeed, I've had a couple of people say they found them enjoyable. All I can say is that for me they've been sickening; and I think it's very important to make clear, to oneself and also to one's colleagues, what it is that he finds sickening. Finally, it is *not* the appearance of uniforms in Harvard Yard — distasteful as that was, painful as it was to see that serene old building being mauled over by police; what was sickening to me was, as I say, not uniforms, but faces — a large number of faces radiating what I can only call the bigotry of ignorance. And I gather that a number of people are now going around saying that 'storm troopers' have entered University Hall. My reply is that storm troopers have indeed entered University Hall, but they didn't do it Thursday morning — they did it Wednesday noon."

Pusey was more restrained in his self-defense. He said: "I think I would like to say to this faculty that to all of us the issue was not any of the demands that the people had made. It really was what we've talked about now for several years in this faculty — freedom within the University: the fact that people cannot use force or violence to interfere with the normal workings of our activity. And to have picked on that symbolic building — but less important as symbol here than the fact that it was the nerve center of the central major faculty of the University — did pose the issue very, very sharply. That being the case, it seemed to me that the alternative chosen was the proper one to take. The decision was not reached quickly; it had been explored over a long period of time. But in the end the president was, of course, the one that had to say go ahead, and that's what I did."

A few speeches condemned the takeover. These were impassioned but brief, and their brevity suggested how pained many faculty members were by events. Most of the more conservative faculty members were ordinary middle-class citizens who had earned their place at Harvard by hard work and ambition, not by accidents of a privileged birth. Once inside the institution, they became it; Harvard was their life. From the point of view of the New England and East Coast aristocracy who preceded them, they were still outsiders. Yet they seemed more attached to the University than those who had built it, and they felt personally injured when it was attacked. Robert McClosky, professor of government, said of the students' behavior: "I felt as if I had been raped."

The day's most stirring speech came from Alexander Gerschenkron, professor of economics, who was one of Harvard's many European refugee professors, and who spoke out of that experience. Several faculty members were European Jews who had fled the Nazis and had come to American universities only twenty years earlier. They seemed to conflate the mobs they had witnessed and suffered from in Europe with the Harvard students, thus they had less understanding of the psychology and moral texture of the protestors. Yet they also had a much greater understanding of the fragility of institutions.

By coincidence, Gerschenkron's remarks followed those of Nobelist economist Wassily Leontief and Nobelist chemist George Kistiakowsky, who had designed the detonator on the atomic bomb. Gerschenkron began lightheartedly, though with a crack that he knew would needle Pusey: "Mr. President, I am afraid that you are now condemned to hear a third exotic interpretation of the Harvard accent."

Then, looking very old and small as he stood, he gave a lecture from the heart. "I am not Pollyanna," he said, reaching a peroration after many minutes extolling academic freedom and praising Pusey's decision as well. "I know quite well that there are things that are horribly wrong with the United States, but I also know that there are many things that are wonderfully right with the United States. Amongst those things are the great universities, and among them is Harvard. There is nothing comparable, there is no counterpart to it anywhere in the world. And to try to destroy, to disrupt, to attack this University is criminal. They attack the University simply because it is in their proximity, just as a criminal steals something just because it is lying there. And in attacking the University they attack the finest flower of American culture.

"Your trouble is that you have not studied the literature of the subject. I am not going to give you a long reading list, but I must summarize for you one single item on that reading list. This is a fairy tale by Hans Christian Andersen, a fairy tale which, in the dark days of the Nazi occupation, the Danes used so subtly and so effectively. That fairy tale is called 'The Most Unbelievable Thing.' There was a kingdom, and in the kingdom there was a king, and he had a princess, and he was interested in the progress of arts. And at a certain point he announced that he would give the princess in marriage to the man who would accomplish the most unbelievable thing.

"And there was great excitement and tremendous competition in the land. Finally, the great day came when all those prepared works had to be presented for judgment. There were many marvelous things, but towering high above them was a truly wonderful thing. It was a clock, a clock produced by a handsome young man. It had a most wonderful mechanism, showing the calendar back and forth into the past and into the future, showing the time, and around the clock were sculptured all the great spiritual and intellectual figures in the history of mankind.

"And whenever the clock struck, those figures exercised most graceful movements. And everybody, the people and the judges, said that yes, to accomplish a thing like that was most unbelievable. And the princess looked at the clock and then looked at the handsome young man, and she liked them both very much. And the judges were just about to pronounce their formal judgment, when a new competitor appeared, a lowbrow fellow. He, too, carried something in his hand, but it was not a work of art, it was a sledgehammer. He walked up to the clock and he swung out and with three blows he smashed up the clock. And everybody said, why, to smash up such a clock, this is surely the most unbelievable thing, and that was how the judges had to adjudge."

Gerschenkron concluded: "I can only hope that the spirits of this faculty will rise and smash up all the criminal nonsense that is going around the campuses of the country. . . . This University, like the clock in the story, like all great works of art, is a frail and fragile creation, and unless you do something about it, this wonderful work of art will be destroyed, and the guilt will be yours."

There were other speeches, some of them praising but most condemning Pusey's actions. In the end, the faculty voted almost unanimously to drop criminal charges against those who had seized University Hall. That ought to have taken the matter away from civil authority and put it in the University's hands.

But Cambridge judge Edward M. Viola ruled that the arrested demonstrators must stand trial for criminal trespass, in spite of Harvard's formal request that charges be dropped. Viola brought in the voice of the world outside protected universities. In his view a crime had been committed and was subject to the state's reaction. Until his ruling, the great majority at Harvard, no matter what sides were taken, still thought of everything that had happened as above the law. At the same April 11 meeting, a resolution was passed criticizing both the seizure of University Hall and the calling in of the police.

Its most significant resolution — one that changed the course of events for the next two months — was one calling for a special faculty committee to be elected to review and act on the incidents. This was what became known as the Committee of Fifteen. Its three-part charge was to write up a history of the events that spring; to make recommendations for the University's future "governance" (an elegant word that cropped up on the spot); and to discipline the students involved in the takeover. Voting the committee into existence, the faculty split down political lines to produce a near-equal number of liberal- and conservative-minded members. The much-lobbied election produced secret pacts and trade-offs. Certain professors were "acceptable," others out of the question. It was the first of many opportunities for faculty members to settle scores with enemies and reward their friends.

The Committee of Fifteen vote also produced two faculty caucuses, liberal and conservative, which now began to meet several days a week. The caucuses watched the committee to ensure that their different views were adequately represented. Everyone quickly became suspicious of everyone else.

The reason that the Committee of Fifteen, which was finally elected at the faculty meeting on April 17, was so important was that it represented the wresting of power from the administration. In a way, it was the faculty's direct and formal statement of contempt. The Ad Board wanted to keep control of the situation, but the faculty would not let it. The assumption prevailed that this disruption was a faculty matter — meaning that only the faculty were capable of dealing with it. The faculty, after all, it was implied, were the real Harvard; the administration, the hired help.

In the end it would not have mattered which group, deans or faculty, would be assigned to clean up the mess. The mess was not to be cleaned up — not in the spring of 1969, not at Harvard, and not in the rest of the country. But by seizing the moment as its own, the faculty became an important part of the story. How they would behave — the decisions they would make that spring — would show a great deal of how they thought about education, the University, the students, and themselves. They would also learn that, whether they liked it or not, they were seen by the students as not all that different from, that is, not superior to, the administration. On the whole, both groups were regarded contemptuously as older people in power.

Since the ancient generations of Harvard bluebloods were dead or were about to die or had lost interest in doing anything but huffing and puffing, it had fallen to the generation of outsiders — faculty and administration alike — to keep the venerable old place intact. But the faculty had no practice in doing that, even if there had been the will. And the administration, which had the will, had little else. We called ourselves Harvard, but we weren't Harvard. We were merely Harvard's current superintendents. We were not members of a ruling class, merely their surrogates; and in any case, the ruling class was fading. By the mid-1970s most universities would decide that the institutions should be led by managers rather than by visionaries or loftier intellectuals. (Other kinds of American corporations would make similar decisions in the 1980s.) But in the spring of 1969, one set of incompetents opposed another.

In the beginning, though, a lot of hope resided in the Committee of Fifteen. Among the senior members were some of the more distinguished faculty: the economist John Dunlop, who later became Ford's secretary of labor; professor of government James Q. Wilson, author of *The Moral Sense* and other books; Alan Heimert; Milton Katz, a noted scholar of international law who later advised President Carter on human rights issues; the venerable biologist John Edsall; Donald Anderson, a professor of applied mathematics; Stanley Hoffmann; and Benjamin Schwartz, a professor of history and government. All were respected teachers and scholars. There was also a member of the physics department, a historian of science named Gerald Holton, who proved himself an indefatigable backroom politician. There were four students and two junior faculty members. I was one of them.

Suddenly I became a known figure at Harvard. I walked into the faculty meeting after the election and was greeted warmly by people who had never spoken to me before. They told me that I had been elected as the Liberal Caucus's boy. Galbraith, at six-foot-seven both a towering and a stooping figure among the left-leaning side of the faculty, looked me over and, I think, found me wanting. Holton, whom I had never met, phoned me the very night of the election to attempt to secure my vote for Stanley Hoffmann, his friend, as chairman of the new committee. (It turned out that the committee would decide to have no chairman; Milton Katz ran the meetings.) Two reporters from the *New York Times* came to write a profile of me as the fair-haired boy, beloved by students and colleagues.

In the midst of all this attention, I decided to give up smoking. Although I played basketball and baseball in high school and college, and continued to play basketball in a ridiculously competitive Harvard Law School league made up of disgruntled ex-jocks, I had always smoked at least two packs of Marlboros a day from the age of fourteen. Even after a game, I would blithely fill the little free space left in my lungs with smoke. But I awoke one morning and told myself that I would try to go without a cigarette till lunchtime and see what happened.

I had lunch with John Kelleher in Harvard Square. Kelleher always boasted that he had quit smoking several times and was looking forward to more. After we had eaten, he lit up, and I, too, lit up. Then he lit up another one. I thought: Stop now or die. So I stopped for good. It was, perhaps, my one and only self-preserving instinct that spring. We had a second child on the way; perhaps that was the reason. Or maybe I simply chose to test my will in a context where I could win — as compared to the one I had just been elected to.

The other business of the April 17 faculty meeting was to pass a resolution limiting the privileges of ROTC to those of any extracurricular organization. This resolution, proposed by the child psychologist Jerome S. Bruner, was important. It, too, represented a rebuke of Pusey — though, in fact, it was little more than a confirmation of what the faculty had voted months earlier. But to the striking students it seemed a concession and a sign of their victory. On the morning of April 18, the Corporation voted to abide by the faculty decision.

On the afternoon of April 18, five days after Ginny's twenty-eighth birthday and one day before Amy's arrival in the world, Ginny and I sat on a stone bench in the Dunster House courtyard, watching Carl push his toy cars in the dirt. Except for an occasional tutor passing by, we were alone within the red-brick walls. All the students in Dunster House, most of the students at Harvard, some thirty-five hundred, were, at that time, gathered in Harvard Stadium on the far side of the Charles River for a massive rally to decide whether or not they would continue to strike for the remainder of the term. Because of the faculty vote on ROTC, they voted to return to classes, but they were still enraged about the bust and, as always, the war.

From our bench Ginny and I could hear the voices of individual speakers, some shrill, some somber, rolling out over loudspeakers, exhorting the students to one action or another. Echoes spilled out across the river, giving all the speeches an instant reprise. Moderate voices were greeted

with boos and catcalls; the fiercer voices, with wild, pro-
longed cheers.

Then someone decided to read aloud the names of the
individual members of the Committee of Fifteen, in whose
hands, they knew, lay the fate of the students involved in
the takeover. Each name received a thunder of boos or an
indeterminate mutter. Only one name, when it was read
aloud, was followed by a cheer so boisterous and long-
lasting, it sounded like an ocean rising over the walls of the
stadium, across the river and into Cambridge and the Dunster House courtyard.

When Ginny and I heard my name and that terrifying
ovation, we looked at each other with the same idiotic
smile on our faces and said nothing. I knew then that I was
a goner.

CHAPTER 5

I OUGHT TO EXPLAIN how an obscure instructor of English came to be accorded both the trust and approval of his colleagues and the roaring cheers of the student body. I ought to do so here because a year later, my elevation was going to increase. I would be appointed Master of Dunster House, the youngest house master in Harvard's history, and my name would appear on the short list for the Harvard presidency — to succeed Pusey, at age twenty-nine. My picture would be in *Newsweek* as one of the final candidates. A poem predicting my selection would appear in the *Boston Globe*.

Three years later, I would be driving away from Harvard, having effectively been fired — that is, denied tenure. I would be shunned or ignored by much of the faculty. I would be reviled by many of the students. April 17 marked the beginning of my rise and of my fall. I deserved much of the fall and none of the rise.

The explanation for my momentary exaltation in 1969

was a combination of charm, insincerity, and an extraordinary amount of luck. I had come to Harvard partly to prove to my father, and I suppose to myself as well, that I was not the goof-off and academic disgrace that I had shown myself to be in grade school, high school, and throughout half of college.

During most of my years at Friends Seminary, the Quaker private school on 16th Street and Stuyvesant Park in New York, to which many parents living in Gramercy Park sent their children, I had done nothing but get into trouble and get bad grades. In high school, I had ranked second from the bottom of my class. Another boy occupied the absolute bottom, but that was because he hardly ever came to school. I came to school every day — for sports, girls, and fooling around. I was tossed out of so many classes (for drawing cartoons and wearing an eyeglass case on my nose) that I eventually gave up going to the principal's office (I reasoned, Why bother him again?) and went directly to the locker room, which became my second home. In my senior year the only college to accept me was N.Y.U.'s College of Arts and Sciences — a small, New Englandish college in the Bronx and the most selective of N.Y.U.'s undergraduate schools, though hardly the Ivy League. I'm not quite sure how I got in even there.

My "who cares?" attitude about studies enraged my father, a much-respected internist and chief of medicine at Doctors Hospital, whom I loved deeply but grudgingly, and with whom I had a long war on many fronts. He who had worked his way up from the semi-ghetto of St. Mark's Place on lower Second Avenue to Gramercy Park and then to upper Fifth Avenue — every step north a leap in class — could not comprehend why his eldest son, who had been given "every advantage," was so determined a failure.

I nearly killed him with surprise in my junior year at N.Y.U. by getting all A's and rising from somewhere around 200th in my class of 250 to number eight. I had decided to see if I could reform, sort of like a game. So fierce and unrelenting was the war between my father and me that, on the day I received my year's top grades, I laid the report in front of him at dinner as if it were an animal killed in a hunt and walked away from the table without saying a word.

Once I saw what the unusual act of opening a book could accomplish, I kept it up. I graduated with honors, published a poem, and won N.Y.U.'s creative-writing prize for a short story. I was offered scholarships for graduate work in English at Princeton, Brown, Columbia, and Michigan, but when the Harvard acceptance came in, the choice was made.

From that point on, everything looked golden. I came to Harvard with a definite, if conventional plan: I would study to get a Ph.D. and become a university professor somewhere, so that I could become a writer. I would have three summer months off a year to write. Lacking the self-confidence to go out and write full-time, I would give myself the safety net of a university and the satisfactions and the distinction of a teacher's life.

Practically from the moment I entered Harvard as a graduate student in the fall of 1962, good things befell me. When I first got there, I knew no one. I knew almost nothing about the professors and their courses. I made up my program of study by wandering into classes that looked interesting from their descriptions in the catalogue.

So it was that I wound up taking Modern British and American Poetry, which was taught by John L. Sweeney, a stunningly gifted teacher who was also a dead ringer for the character actor Edmund Gwenn, the Santa Claus of *Miracle on 34th Street*. Not only did Jack Sweeney teach me how to teach, how to encourage students to speak creatively; but also, when he retired, he bequeathed me his course, which I had been teaching on April 9.

I met Kelleher by wandering into a seminar he was offering on eighteenth-century poets. I knew and cared nothing about eighteenth-century poets, but I needed to fulfill a seminar requirement, and Kelleher — because a vacancy had suddenly opened up — accepted me. In him I found the man I wanted to attach myself to at Harvard. He was the wisest and most complete teacher and dedicated scholar I had ever seen. It wasn't his brains or learning that drew me to him. Or his abilities as a teacher. His near-confounding stammer drove most students away; it was discouraging and, at times, heartbreaking to see him struggle with his tongue, as if it were a snake filling his mouth, merely to get it to lie still and allow him to speak his mind.

Rather, his attractiveness lay in his character and in his hard-nosed view of life and history. There was no bunk about him. He came from an Irish family in the mill city of Lawrence, Massachusetts. He had gone out for boxing at Dartmouth. He was a handsome man, squarely built at about five-foot-ten, with a serious, straightforward face and a helmet of white hair. He could have just as happily been a cop or a postal clerk like his father. He was a first-class carpenter who embodied the carpenter's dictum, "Measure twice, cut once." He condemned European Romantics "for thinking that they were ten feet tall"; he felt that "Romanticism led to Dachau." His view of the eighteenth century, in contrast, was that people then knew that they were people-sized — powerless before nature, corruptible, mortal. Since his field was Irish history and literature, I decided to make it my field, too.

In the spring of 1963, Ginny and I were married in a Unitarian church in New York to which we had been attracted because it dedicated a pew to a cat. That summer we settled in our first apartment, in Cambridge, five furnished rooms ($150 per month with heat) on the first floor of a gray frame house on Wendell Street, about a quarter of a mile north of the Yard. The sister of former speaker of the house Tip O'Neill lived around the corner on Oxford Street, though at the time O'Neill was just a popular local politician. It was a blue-collar neighborhood, as was most

71

of Cambridge, with a few students mixed in. Generally, the people were nice and friendly, especially to us, who, in spite of Harvard, looked like the all-American couple.

I won a full scholarship for my second year. This was nothing special; scholarships were plentiful in those days. In my application I had to note my father's income, which was high and would probably disqualify anyone from a scholarship nowadays. But I wrote simply that "I no longer wish to depend on my parents for my schooling." In the flush 1960s that was sufficient.

I also had a teaching fellowship in freshman English, called Gen Ed A, that paid $2,000 — a fortune. But Ginny really supported us, and she did this by achieving the un-thinkable. In Cambridge, Massachusetts, where you only got jobs in the public sector if you knew the right person, and where it didn't hurt to be Irish, my beautiful, sweet-natured, Episcopalian wife got a job teaching in the public schools, easy as pie. She walked in to the school board, dazzled them with her skill and her integrity, and walked out with a position teaching second grade at the Haggerty School in West Cambridge. Her salary was $6,000. With my money and hers, we were rolling in dough, and — in the ratio of expenses to income, as Mr. Bumble would say — we were never as rich again.

That first summer of our marriage and the two years following constituted the kind of idyll that young couples are supposed to experience but rarely do. Ginny was adored at the Haggerty School, where the students came from mostly Irish and Italian working-class families who wanted their kids to learn. I watched her teach there. She taught six- and seven-year-olds to read. It was like watching a musician — not merely a gifted technician, but one who could lose herself in the music. She and her subject were inseparable; the children were enthralled with both at once. And her confidence, which she did not always evidence with adults, was picked up by the children. They knew that they were in the presence of someone they could trust with their lives.

Our friends were other graduate students, both married and single. We went to one another's homes for dinner, groused and dreamed and drank lots of inexpensive wine. We played banjos and guitars and sang folk songs. We watched the Celtics beat the Knicks every time and were the only two people in Boston Garden cheering for the Knicks. The crowd booed the two of us. We saw the second Muhammad Ali–Sonny Liston fight on a large screen in Boston Garden. We played tennis on the Cambridge courts. We went to the old movies, like *Casablanca*, before it became cultish to do so. We bought a car. We drove up to Crane Beach in Ipswich, north of Boston, and ended hot, long days at a diner biting into lobster rolls cooked in butter.

The evenings during our first summer of married life, we would sit on our back porch in Wendell Street licking ice cream cones and listening to a couple of girls in a nearby house sing "Peas, peas, eating goober peas." That was our life. We watched the sun drop like a bloody egg, went into our tiny bedroom, made love, and fell asleep.

In those years, everyone handed me everything. Once, on the Fourth of July, Ginny and I went down to the Charles for a picnic with two other married graduate school friends. Kids and their folks milled about on the shore. Boats sailed by, festooned with symbols of America. The sky was lit in the distance with the silent bouquets of fireworks. I was expounding on some uninteresting idea to my three unrapt listeners, holding a fried chicken leg in my hand and gesticulating with the thing as if it were a pointer. Suddenly, a four-year-old towhead waddled by, saw the chicken leg, snatched it out of my hand, and waddled on. The kid believed that he was born to take chicken legs from the hands of strangers, that the world was bursting with chicken legs waiting only for his arrival. I understood him perfectly.

The following Sunday, Ginny and I wandered down to the Charles by ourselves, just to sit. We had been disappointed the night before because we'd gone to a Bob Dylan concert at Brandeis, but Dylan had never showed. The river was unusually quiet in the early morning. There were only two other people nearby — a slightly built man lazily strumming a guitar, and a striking woman with shoulder-length black hair sitting Indian-style in front of him. Ginny and I approached. Joan Baez signaled us to sit. The guitarist played and sang "Tambourine Man" long before he recorded it. We sang along.

I wandered into everything, and everything good or entertaining came to me. I attended my first poetry reading one late fall afternoon, because I happened to be passing Boylston Hall in the old Yard. John Berryman was reading his recent "Henry" poems to a Harvard audience he clearly was afraid of and whom he also clearly despised. In the audience sat Professor Harry Levin, whose stiff, aristocratic bearing was due equally to genuine intellectual superiority, genuine intellectual snobbiness, and to the fact that he was half-deaf. For some reason — perhaps he had been a student of Harry's — Berryman bristled at the sight of Levin, who was sitting only a few rows back from the stage, next to his wife, Elena. I sat in the back and had an excellent view of the show to follow.

Berryman, who was as mad as he appeared, looked as if he had just emerged from a wind tunnel — his tie and jacket flung off-center, his hair standing up in spikes. He had not gotten five lines into his reading when he stopped suddenly and surveyed the crowd. "You know," he looked up menacingly, "this stuff is funny! Hilarious, really. Why aren't you laughing?" Once instructed that the poem was funny, people began to laugh uproariously at every line. This contented Berryman only for a few minutes. Then he stopped and again looked out into the audience at Harry Levin. Levin was sitting ramrod straight, staring at Berryman.

"You bug me, Harry!" Berryman shouted. Levin sat motionless. There were a few gasps, then everyone fell silent.

"You *bug* me, Harry," said Berryman again. Still no reaction from Harry.

"Harry!" Berryman yelled. "Harry! You bug me!" At that, Elena Levin mercifully leaned over and spoke loudly into the better ear of her husband, who, of course, had not heard a word that Berryman said. "Harry?" she called out. "He says you bug him." Whereupon, showing no emotion whatever, Levin rose from his seat and, with Elena at his side, left the hall.

"That's better," said Berryman, and the reading continued.

In the academic year 1964–65, I took to writing poems. I was accepted in Robert Lowell's poetry-writing seminar — more luck still, since I got in on the strength of the only poem I had completed that year. Getting into Lowell's seminar was an embrace by the literary pantheon.

I won a Fulbright scholarship to Ireland in 1965, where I practically was given my entire Ph.D. dissertation. I started out planning to do research for a dissertation on the playwright John Millington Synge, but in the middle of the year I came across a memoir by a friend of Synge's named Stephen MacKenna, a Dublin journalist and the great translator of Plotinus. I got sufficiently interested in MacKenna that I decided to do my dissertation on him instead. In a typically lucky episode, the man who had done the preface to MacKenna's memoir, E. R. Dodds, Regius Professor of Greek at Oxford, simply gave me all the original MacKenna papers in his possession. I wrote him stating my interest; he invited me over to Oxford from Dublin; I spent an hour talking with him over two tall gins; and he handed me my Ph.D.

Carl was conceived in Ireland — during our first week of trying, of course. We decided to return to New York for his birth, because we were leery of his being born in a nursing home, which was the custom in Ireland. True to the Irish sense of humor, the baby nursing homes in Dublin were located on Hatch Street. Besides, my father was a bigwig at Doctors Hospital in New York, so we knew all would go well there, which it did. The McNamara incident occurred shortly after we returned with our new baby to Cambridge after the summer of 1966, at which time another lucky event happened.

The director of Gen Ed A, Robert Kiely, was about to take a year's leave of absence, starting in the fall of 1966. I had been a teaching fellow in Gen Ed A since my second year in graduate school. Kiely asked me if I would serve as acting director of the program, which entailed heading a staff of some sixty teaching fellows and a student enrollment of fourteen hundred. I had no idea why he chose me to do it, except that I looked reliable, and since everything was being handed to me anyway, why not this? Gen Ed A was a loathsome requirement of every freshman at Harvard; the students felt superior to it; the teaching fellows felt inferior to the students. But things at Harvard generally run themselves, and I figured that if I looked pleasant and attentive, and was just inventive enough to do a few harmless things without appearing radically reformist, I would be okay. And so I was. People on the English faculty kept telling me what a great job I was doing, mainly because nothing fell apart.

Then, one afternoon in that same fall of 1966, I was walking along Massachusetts Avenue, south of the Yard, when I heard my name called. "Are you Mr. Rosenblatt?" (It was a question I never answered too quickly after the McNamara business.) Behind me stood Jere Whiting, whose visage and reputation were so severe, I had always done my best to stay out of his range. What he wanted to know was if my family and I would be good enough to live in his home — rent free — while he took *his* year of absence. "We'll pay for the heat, of course," he added. "Couldn't ask you to do that. It's a big house." It was, in fact, a big, beautiful frame house on Walker Street, in the heart of Radcliffe.

Such an offer could not have come out of the blue, though such was my good fortune in those days that I hardly questioned it. With Ginny planning to stop teaching for at least a year to take care of Carl, we had almost no money except for the little extra I was going to be paid for running Gen Ed A. What I later learned was that Kelleher had mentioned to his friend Whiting that we were a respectable couple who needed housing.

Suddenly, then, at the age of twenty-five, I was a new father, the director of the largest academic program in the College, and the occupant of an elegant home in Cambridge. After the fall of 1966, there was also that bit of mystery about me. Was I not also the man who had put his body in front of Secretary McNamara's car? Was I not someone to notice, someone to reckon with, a potential leader of men? The answer to those questions was no, but only I knew that for sure.

In the spring of 1967, I was appointed Senior Tutor in Dunster House. This was not one of those goodies that fell into my lap; I actively sought the job. A fellow student of Kelleher's, Don Akenson, held this plum of a position before I did, and he wanted to move on, to become a real scholar. So I asked him to recommend me as his successor. He did this gladly, since we were friends, but he also warned me that getting the appointment would be an uphill fight because I was a Jew. The Master of Dunster House at the time, Alwin Pappenheimer, affectionately called Papp, a distinguished biologist from a family of distinguished biologists, was also a Jew, though he was not reared as one; and in his deepest, if confused, heart, he wanted desperately to be thought of as a flinty, old-line New England Protestant. He married a Forbes, a lovely, perceptive, slightly pixilated woman named Pauline. He worked at becoming a good squash player. He played horseshoes. Every morning before dawn, there was Papp sculling on the Charles, even in the dead of winter, proving (to God knows whom) that his blood was as blue as his face.

Of all things on earth, he did not want his Senior Tutor — one of the more visible and influential positions at Harvard — to represent a return to the shtetl. What persuaded him, in the end, to hire me, after a long, prayerful search for someone more suitable, was that I looked and acted more WASPy than he did. My prep-schoolish voice was perfect. My physical features were unidentifiable. For a Jew, I had a fairly straight nose. I had social graces. I was an athlete. I came from the Gramercy Park neighborhood of New York. Best of all, perhaps, my wife was high-born and beautiful; she would always enter a room ahead of me.

The thing that finally swung his decision in my favor, however, was his discovery — after numerous awkward interviews — that I was only a little more Jewish than he was. What he could not know was that, while I too was reared in an areligious family, I was very Jewish in my reflexive loyalties, that I had chosen to have an Orthodox bar mitzvah specifically because my family was areligious, and that while such acts were driven more by orneriness than faith, I was a Jew in my bones. Papp could not see my bones. As long as I did not arrive at Dunster House behind a pushcart, that was good enough for him.

It was as Senior Tutor that I first saw and dealt with people in trouble, and that I realized I had a definite, if superficial, gift for making them feel better. Most Harvard students did well academically (the joke went that Harvard grades ran the gamut from A to B), but most, too, were shaken and nerve-racked. My conversations with undergraduates who would come to my office ostensibly to talk about getting into law school or medical school (in those days no one admitted wanting to go to business school) would often wind up with them talking about their girl-friends or their fear of the draft and their desire to leave college and take up roots in the New Hampshire woods. The menace of Vietnam had something to do with their state of mind, but not everything. They knew that they were coming to manhood at a time when everything in America was up for grabs, and they were young. In the re-sentful fury that was often aroused in adults in the late 1960s at what looked like a horde of bearded Vikings attack-ing the national soul, it was easy to forget that these Vikings were seventeen, eighteen, and nineteen years of age.

My ability to soothe their worries was solely verbal, thus misleading both to them and to me. As Senior Tutor I developed a reputation as an effective advocate for stu-dents who got into trouble with the Ad Board. It was said that I could get a kid off for anything short of murder, but in truth the ethos of the Ad Board was such that it was the very rare case that received any serious punishment. An old trick of the Senior Tutors and freshman deans, which I quickly picked up, was to allow the discussion of a student in trouble to go on as if one intended to throw the book at him. Say, for example, that a student named Fred had been on academic probation for two terms running, and in the current term he had gotten nearly all failing grades yet again. It was the routine of the Senior Tutor to let every-one rail at Fred as a lazy dope, deserving of immediate ex-pulsion. Then the Senior Tutor would weigh in, heaving with disgust and hurling scorn at the wastrel, Fred. At the end of his remarks, however, the Senior Tutor would slip in something like the following: "In conclusion, I cannot see how we can keep Fred in school. And I do not think that we should take his mother's illness into consideration at all."

There would follow a sudden flurry of questions about Fred's mother's illness. And perhaps her rheumatoid arthritis did indeed have a distracting effect on Fred's work. And Fred did get *one* C, after all, and *one* professor did attest that Fred was not the *stupidest* student he had ever taught. In the end, Fred was allowed to stay, with all sorts of dire warnings attached to his record. The Senior Tutor would very reluctantly allow the Ad Board to be so lenient and would express his opinion, in the sternest terms, that this would be Fred's very last chance.

Everyone knew that there was only one thing harder than getting into Harvard and that was getting out.

I also earned the reputation as sympathetic to students in the antiwar effort, and, in a sort of dispassionate way, I was. What concerned me more was the anguish of the students opposing the war. When they burned their draft cards, they would get into fights with their parents and ask me to intercede, which I did. I signed a petition of teaching fellows stating that we supported the right of students to burn their draft cards in protest against the war. Sanford Levinson, a Dunster House tutor in government and now a professor at the University of Texas, who had become well known for writing an article, with Doris Kearns, on

"How to Dump Johnson," expressed some worry to me that by signing the petition we were abetting an illegal act. He was rightly concerned that we could get into trouble. But I was cool, as the kids said. "Sandy," I asked him, "are our lives so exciting that we can't stand a little more?"

Generally, I was developing the reputation of "a guy you could go to for help" — Al Gore had said that to Peretz — not only among the students in and out of Dunster House, but among the faculty as well. Indeed, starting in late 1967, I was making a name for myself in the University as a man of feeling without my being aware of it. It was the kind of reputation that always sounds better than it is and for which one eventually pays a price.

One student in the House was irretrievably troubled. The only child of a farm family in the Midwest, he had come to Harvard against the wishes of his father, who deemed it unseemly to go to college at all, much less a place as godless and wicked as Harvard. He was blond and pale and very quiet. He lived a near-solitary existence in the House, and he had tried to kill himself twice in his freshman year. He had been sent to a mental hospital. Released after a year, he reentered Harvard at the time I joined Dunster House, and he came to talk to me from time to time, almost always about studies, nothing personal.

One morning in early April 1968, the University police called me to the boy's room. He had swallowed cyanide, which he had cooked up in a chem lab; this was the attempt that took. Pappenheimer asked me if I would phone the parents; Papp wasn't up to doing things like that, and he was self-aware enough to know it. I had no idea if I was up to it either, but it had to be done. I gulped and dialed the number. The boy's father answered. When I told him what had happened, there was a pause. Then he said: "Well, we aren't going to pay to ship the body home."

The boy's diary contained so many entries expressing his painful hatred of his parents, I decided not to send it home with him. There was also an entry about me: "Spoke with Mr. Rosenblatt again. Feel better."

That spring of 1968, since I was about to receive my Ph.D., I began to interview for teaching positions. I sent out dozens of letters in hopes that someplace would hire me. I did not have to look long. Yale was about to make me an offer, but then came Harvard. The chairman of the English Department, Walter Jackson Bate, the preeminent biographer of Keats and Johnson, called and asked if I wanted the Briggs-Copeland appointment.

Bate represented all the greatness and the lunacy of the English department as it once had been. A farm boy from Indiana, he had gone to the College and to the Graduate School on scholarships, and he became one of an entirely new breed of English professors — those who worked for pay, as opposed to those who had come from wealthy families and taught college to have something respectable to do. He told me that when he was a young instructor, he barely was paid enough to live on, so he went to the department chairman, who came from one of those old, rich families, to state his plight. The elder man was sympathetic. He told Bate: "These are hard times, Jack. You'll have to dip into capital."

He looked like a haggard old salt who had barely survived a squall, and he spoke in a long, flat Midwestern accent that sounded like one long complaint.

"Raahger," he began. "Do you know about the Briggs-Copeland appointment?"

"No," I said.

"Waal," again taking forever, "it's what we give once in a while to an instructor to teach those creative writing courses." I ignored his condescension, but I was still not following him.

"Waal," he went on, "we wondered if you'd be interested in becoming the Briggs-Copeland Instructor next year."

I did not have to think it over. "Of course, Jack," I said.

"Waal, Maynard Mack says he wants you at Yale."

"Jack, I . . ."

"You'll have to teach those writing courses."

"Jack . . ."

"What do you say?" he asked.

"I say yes, Jack."

"Waal, that's good," he said, his voice fading away. I ran downstairs to tell Ginny.

"My God!" she said. "You're an instructor at Harvard. Who woulda thunk it!"

"You!" I told her, and kissed her as hard as I could.

I was the only person given a faculty appointment in English from the graduate school. There were several classmates who were more qualified and who had done much better in school. But I was considered a good boy and was known to have an interest in writing, and there was this chair they had to fill.

So there I was. I would be entering the academic year 1968–69 as a member of the faculty of Harvard University and as Senior Tutor of Dunster House. Everything good that could happen was happening to Ginny and me. At commencement, the undergraduate degrees were given out in the Houses in a nice ceremony, more intimate than the convocation in the Yard. I elected to receive my doctorate in the House as well, and Pappenheimer "hooded" me on the platform in the Dunster House courtyard. In my bright crimson robe, I gave a speech congratulating the seniors — and also eulogizing a Dunster House student, whom I had not known, who had been killed in Vietnam that spring. No matter how happy the occasion, the war was never far from the University.

Soon, the graduates and their families packed up their cars and went home, and Cambridge became a sleepy village. Ginny and I had the languid summer to look forward to, playing with Carl and considering the future. There was not much to consider. The future had been coming to us with so many gifts, I began to feel that it was my lot to sit back and receive good news.

The fall came and went. The student activists were growing more agitated, but I was fairly unconcerned. We were on the same side, after all. Reason would always prevail, and the war would have to end sometime. I taught my writing courses and I looked forward to teaching Sweeney's modern poetry course in the spring. The House was running well. Best of all, Ginny was pregnant again. Nothing could go wrong.

On a frigid afternoon in December, I went over to Bill Alfred's house to talk. Bill was not yet back from class, so I sat with his father, a hard Brooklyn Irishman, and listened to his stories for an hour or so. We hadn't bothered to turn on the lights. At about five, Bill came home, looked at us, and asked his father: "Why are you sitting in the dark?" His father replied: "I don't want him to see that I'm telling him lies."

CHAPTER 6

I T WAS AS SENIOR TUTOR that I began to get involved in the political activity that led up to the University Hall takeover, and to gain the first understanding of some of the ideas and attitudes that underlay the student-University war and that eventually brought Harvard and its students to University Hall.

It is odd to remember, but the wild-in-the-streets sixties were also a time when the ideal of the Harvard gentleman was still in force. People told a story about a Harvard tutor, sometime around World War I, who had observed an undergraduate trying to pick up a girl on the train from New York to Boston. The tutor caught up with the boy at Harvard, demanded to see his bursar's card, and recommended that he be expelled for behaving like a "masher."

As late as 1969, students in the Houses were still required to wear ties and jackets in the dining halls at lunch and dinner — the so-called coat-and-tie rule. "We wore gray coats and narrow little ties," John Updike (class of

1954) recalled, "like apprentice deacons." Many of them complied with the rule. Others who did not were spoken to. And while it was generally recognized that this formality was antiquated, its symbolism remained intact. By the end of the sixties, there were students who did not bother to wear a shirt in the dining halls. One cannot overestimate the sense of social deterioration felt by many of the older faculty members when it became clear that fair Harvard would no longer dress at Brooks Brothers.

The matter of dress was, in fact, significant. Kelleher told me: "About costumes. I remember reading a piece in the [*Boston*] *Globe* by a reporter who had interviewed young workmen in East Cambridge. At that time I had thought that all the loud professions of solidarity with the oppressed and exploited workers were uttered in the sheltered confines of the Yard and the nearer part of Oxford Street, and that students took every good care to stay away from East Cambridge or Chelsea or the parts of Somerville where actual living workers might be found. But I was wrong. It seems that some especially sincere graduate students did venture into East Cambridge and make actual contact with genuine workers. According to the article, an odd one to find in the *Globe* [because of its leftist bias], the young workers with whom contact was made were vastly amused not only by the proffers of understanding and solidarity, but by the care the students had taken to come attired in true workers' costume, which according to their notion consisted of brand-new work boots, brand-new checked wool shirts, and real dungarees, not Levi's. The workmen of course wore whatever they felt like on the job. And when they got home, changed into their spiffiest clothes for going out on the town. They couldn't believe these characters, hadn't known that such innocence actually existed. It's sort of sad to think of all that money being spent in the Army and Navy Store down in Central Square, and all for nothing.

"Within the Yard and the Houses, costumes were, as I look back on it, the first signs of the coming storm. You'll remember that the rules required a jacket, a shirt, and a tie in the dining hall. And indeed, up till about 1966 that was what was worn to class. Sam Morison [Samuel Eliot Morison, who wrote the definitive history of Harvard] had been accustomed to order anyone without a jacket or a tie out of his lectures, and had been obeyed. But by this time, Sam was retired. Now, young sea lawyers began to appear who wore a zipper jacket (it was after all a jacket), a t-shirt (philologically a shirt), and around the neck, a shoestring tied. It was about that time, too, that the realization spread that if any lecturer or dining-room employee or House Master tried to do anything about this, he would not be backed up by the administration. No more use demanding to see an offender's bursar's card. I can remember one smug character dressed in the full pain-in-the-ass costume, coming in and sitting in an aisle seat. And another touch, a more significant one, he was drinking coffee or something from a Styrofoam cup. As I was about to leave the room, I saw that in departing he had set the cup neatly on the floor. That was the first time I ever saw that done, but it has persisted ever since. As I said, 'Do your own thing. And let somebody else clean up after you.' "

In short, the change of dress code was not only a way for students to say to their elders, "We do not look like you." It also was a way of saying "We are not you," and may have also meant "We are against you."

As late as 1969, as well, "parietals" were in force. Parietals — a word that was invented at Harvard, I think — referred to the rule that a young woman was not allowed in a young man's House room after 11 P.M. My first year as Senior Tutor was Al Gore's junior year. One night, sometime after midnight, I was returning to Dunster House, and emerging from the House at the same time were Al and his girlfriend, Tipper. There was but one path connecting us and no escape for the future vice president. I saw the terror in his Boy Scout eyes, which might have read: "There goes the presidency." We passed each other quickly on the path. I greeted Al and Tipper: "Good evening, boys."

When the students blocked the McNamara car or trapped the Dow recruiter or sat in at Paine Hall, it was a matter that went to the heart of the Harvard class system. For centuries, it had always been assumed that Harvard endowed its students with class — upper class and, most important, ruling class. Yale might make its little contributions to the foreign service; Princeton, to Wall Street and the oak-paneled law firms. But Harvard governed the country. Bernard de Voto defined the University as "a republic within the Republic." President Charles William Eliot (1869–1909) exhorted students to "Enter to grow in wisdom; Depart to serve thy country and thy kind."

At first, serving the country (or the colony) meant establishing a direct connection with God. Cotton Mather (class of 1678) was the first to state that Harvard had a purpose at all, specifically to be a "College of Divines." From its halls would emerge the New World's ministers, governors, and judges. Mather also connected the College with the city of Cambridge, which he called in Hebrew "Kirjath-Sepher" — the City of the Books. Harvard was to be at once a seminary and a seat of government.

In the eighteenth century, when orthodox Congregationalists held sway, they repeated the line that Harvard was to be a theological entity. But by the nineteenth century a new interpretation of purpose was offered: the school was also charged with providing young gentlemen with a broad general education, to widen their interests and eventually their influence. These two aims were not seen as mutually exclusive. Samuel Eliot Morison, in his monumental *Tercentennial History of Harvard College and University*, wrote that Harvard was to be both a religious college and a school of letters.

Over the years there were struggles over emphasis — lay or Christian — but both aims always took for granted the ultimate goal that Harvard was to lead, and to provide leaders. The historian Bernard Bailyn put it: "[Harvard was] a beachhead on this pagan continent, launched by a task force of Christian militia charged with the divine obligation of forwarding the providential transfer of God's learning from land to land and people to people." While remaining staunchly Christian in structure and spirit, the institution was created to provide first colonial then American leadership of church and state, however separate those entities might be otherwise.

In an odd way, too, it was to be a business, or at least to look more like a business in terms of structure than an institution of learning. The first organizational act that the Master and Fellows of the College did (around 1650) was to form a corporation, thus making Harvard a self-governing institution run by a board of directors that owned property. Harvard is that today. And the Corporation — the oldest such organization in the western world — is composed exactly as it was originally, consisting of the president, the treasurer, and five fellows. It was the Corporation that the University Hall occupiers attacked specifically when they issued their original demands.

Another layer of directors was added, the Board of Overseers, which, while not as powerful as the Corporation in terms of day-to-day decisions, was legally the superior body. Here was yet another demonstration of the Puritan thesis that someone is always looking over someone else. The Board of Overseers provided one more nonacademic level of authority on which the University could draw for anything from a visiting committee to inspect a department, to a committee to deal with a student riot. Both the Corporation and the Overseers, normally quiescent bodies, found more activity than they had ever sought in the spring of 1969.

Finally, there was no individual founder of Harvard College. John Harvard was simply a generous fellow who left the new college his library and half his estate. Instead, the part-religious, part-educational, part-entrepreneurial institution was founded by the Massachusetts legislature. Conceived and supported by the state, and owning property, and running its own affairs, Harvard was from the outset not only a public and private institution; it was a characteristically American one. Long before there was a nation to which the words could be applied, it was of the community by the community and for the community. From its inception, its duty, or in Puritan terms, its task, was to serve both the governmental and the business ambitions of American society, democracy, and capitalism.

From the outbreak of World War II, when the United States government was becoming like a university itself — expanding its departments and its disciplines — Harvard filled those jobs. In the person of President Franklin Del-ano Roosevelt, Harvard was the presidency itself; and when a non–Harvard type like the "haberdasher" Harry Truman slid into the office, he was too low class to be acknowledged. It became an odd standing joke that Harvard would never offer Truman an honorary degree — this from the University that gave an honorary degree to the Shah of Iran, in 1963.

Every administration has filled itself with Harvard appointments. Four Harvard men were members of Nixon's cabinet, two of whom, Pat Moynihan and Henry Kissinger, went to Washington in 1969. The Kennedy administration included McNamara; Secretary of the Treasury Douglas Dillon; Secretary of Labor Willard Wirtz; presidential adviser Richard Neustadt; and Attorney General Robert Kennedy; as well as the head of the National Security Council, McGeorge Bundy; the ambassador to Japan, Edwin O. Reischauer; and Galbraith, who was ambassador to India. There were more Harvard men in the Reagan administration than in Kennedy's. White House advisers Richard Darman, professor of government Samuel Huntington, and economists Dunlop and Martin Feldstein, all of whom were at Harvard in 1969, were later to join that administration. Jim Wilson almost became the head of the FBI under President Carter. The economist Robert Reich was later to serve under President Clinton, as secretary of labor, along with Jamie Gorelick; the director of the budget, Franklin D. Raines; and Al Gore.

One of the reasons that very few people who had gone to Harvard ever have felt any emotional loyalty toward it is that, by design, one's loyalties were supposed to go outward, toward the outer world of power, not inward toward University Hall. What the University called fostering a sense of independence, the students called loneliness; in some instances, abandonment.

Harvard actively encouraged, indeed developed the feeling in the students of being outsiders. After spending eleven years there as student and teacher, and in the twenty-seven years since, in which I have maintained several connections to the place, I rarely met anyone who has spoken of Harvard with real affection. In 1970, James Fallows, author of *Breaking the News,* a criticism of the press, and editor of *U.S. News & World Report,* was president of the *Crimson.* He was very well thought of by students and faculty, and was headed for Oxford as a Rhodes Scholar. Yet he told me: "I view those undergraduate years as the four most unhappy years of my life. The University was almost completely unsupportive of undergraduates. Nobody could care less. I came from a public school in Redlands, California. I met my dorm proctor *once* as a freshman. It was not that I was against the sink-or-swim approach, but in many emotional ways I was sinking. I remember at some opening week ceremony my freshman year the prevailing attitude was 'Well, we'll see how smart you guys are.'"

Tony Lukas recalled his first day at Harvard. He found his room in his freshman dormitory in the Yard, then went to see *The Maltese Falcon,* which was playing in the Square. He had come from the Putney School in Vermont, where "lights out" was at 10 P.M., and as he sat in the movie theater, he eyed a wall clock nervously as the hands approached 10. Scared that the gates to the Yard would be locked, he bolted from the theater. At 9:56 he approached a University policeman standing by the wall of the Yard. "Could you tell me when they lock the gates?" he asked the cop, who responded, "Sonny, you're in the big world now. Those gates are never locked." (Lukas observed that the gates *were* locked the night of the bust.)

What everyone noted is the feeling, and often the dread, of being on one's own. David Halberstam (class of 1955), author of many books, notably *The Best and the Brightest*, said: "I don't know that *unhappy* is the word, but I certainly felt alone for the first time. All these bright, public high school kids in this place. They think: 'Am I good enough? Did they make a mistake?' Then, too, we were children of the meritocracy. There was a sense that Harvard had let us in educationally but not socially. Was this our place?"

"I didn't expect Harvard to take care of me," said Michael Kazin. "I had people taking care of me in the subculture of SDS."

Even the insiders were outsiders. All the men whom the SDS students railed at — Pusey, Ford, and Glimp — came from the Midwest or the Far West. Ford came to Harvard from Minnesota, Glimp from Idaho, Pusey from Iowa. They were devoted to Harvard, sometimes with unrequited love, but they were not the soul of the University. If a soul existed, it lay in such names as Cabot, Adams, Lowell, Peabody, Coolidge, Choate, Perkins, and Lee, alumni and Overseers who were invisible except at commencement, when they would march in procession with their ancestors' ghosts. But these people, too, seemed at a distance from the University. To create ever-widening circles was Harvard's aim, and even he who tossed the first stone into the pond disappeared into a bronze representation that probably bore no likeness to the original. In 1940, David McCord, sort of the official Harvard poet, wrote:

> *"Is that you,*
> *John Harvard?"*
> *I said to his statue.*
> *"Aye — that's me," said John.*
> *"And after you're gone."*

Whatever intellectual standards were applied in letting people into the University, the prevailing emotional standard was to determine that one was capable of making it alone. That standard applied to everything, including the administrative structure. When considering the budgetary concerns of the separate schools in the University, the motto was "Every tub on its own bottom" — a motto invoked by Harvard presidents or treasurers whenever it was suggested that one school could get out of a financial hole by borrowing money from another. For students, "Every tub on its own bottom" often meant that they were set adrift.

Throughout 1969, before the University Hall takeover and the eruptions that followed, the *New Yorker* writer E. J. Kahn lived in the University, gathering material for a book he was planning on Harvard. Wherever he went, people told him that a rampage such as what had occurred at Columbia could never happen at Harvard because of the House system. Sitting across from Kahn in a Cambridge restaurant, I gave him such sage, confident assurances myself. The conventional, and as it turned out thoroughly incorrect, wisdom was that with the College decentralized into individual Houses of three to four hundred students each, there was more personal attention paid each student, thus a greater sense of cohesion and common purpose. That was all untrue. To be sure, there were strong ties created among people within certain Houses, but the Houses themselves were statements of the atomizing of the institution. It was always considered too corny, too rah-rah — too like *ordinary* universities — for Harvard to build a sense of central loyalty.

The Houses were really Potemkin villages posing as centers, or hearts, of the University. There was no heart of the University. Of the two main college songs, one was "Harvardiana," with its repetition of the word "Harvard" sounding like a parody of a college song, and the other, "Fair Harvard," which was a hymn to centrifugal force:

> *Farewell! be thy destinies onward and bright!*
> *To thy children the lesson still give,*
> *With freedom to think, and with patience to bear,*
> *And for right ever bravely to live.*

99

There was no mascot anyone could identify. There was no nickname, except for "the Crimson," which, being a fancy name for a color, was more off-putting than inspiring. There was no college try, or college football rally, or weeping together for good old whatever. The one time I ever saw any communal weeping at Harvard was after University Hall, after the police had been called in and a number of independent Harvard heads had been bloodied.

Rather than creating an institution that was designed to draw on the collective loyalties of its members, Harvard did something quite opposite, and, from one perspective, a great deal more clever. It created a place that played to all shades of independence of each individual — from egotism to true original inventiveness. The reason so many writers have come from Harvard as compared with other institutions is that Harvard gives everybody loneliness, whether they seek it or not. Writers tend to seek it. When Thomas Wolfe wrote of Eugene Gant's Harvard in *Of Time and the River*, he spoke for the breed: "He did not know the moment that it came, but it came instantly, at once. And from that moment on mixed fury seized him, from that moment on, his life, more than the life of any one that he would ever know, was to be spent in solitude and wandering."

The reason that Harvard, in recent years especially, has produced so many well-known journalists is that journalists thrive on hot-shot independence. These individuals, including myself, are so connected to one another in a professional chain as to make the original old-boy network seem quaint. One might wonder why Harvard, the richest university in the world, richer than most countries, with an endowment of over $8 billion, inspires graduates to donate money to it. Part of the answer is that the University has turned the milking of alumni for donations into an art form. But the main reason is that Harvard is useful in practical ways to its graduates, and they are grateful for that. There may be no school spirit of the traditional type, but the mere fact of having a Harvard degree — of being associated with so selective and exclusive a club — has made careers for hundreds of thousands of people.

Harvard did not look inward — except in the sense of every university, of being fascinated by interior concerns and by gossip. It saw itself instead as a hatchery for the best eggs that were destined to cluck and strut into the outer world. John Reed, whose enthrallment with communism produced *Ten Days That Shook the World*, wrote a short memoir of Harvard in 1917, shortly before sailing to Russia. "Harvard under President Eliot was unique," he wrote. "Individualism was carried to the point where a man who came for a good time could get through and graduate without having learned anything." Then he added something true for any era: "Students . . . criticized the faculty for not educating them, attacked the sacred institution of intercollegiate athletics, sneered at undergraduate clubs so holy that no one dared mention their names. No matter what you were or what you did, at Harvard you could find your own kind."

In the eleven years I was there, the undergraduate hatchery produced Kinsley, Fallows, Gorelick, Helprin, Rich, Kazin, Rappaport, Kaplan, and Atlas; Walter Isaacson, the editor of *Time* magazine; Esther Dyson, the cyberspace expert; the actors Stockard Channing and John Lithgow; poets Rachel Hadas and Sydney Goldfarb; playwright Chris Durang, who wrote *Sister Mary Ignatius Explains It All for You*; and the *Saturday Night Live* comedian Al Franken, who wrote the bestselling *Rush Limbaugh Is a Big Fat Idiot*. Both Durang and Franken were students in Dunster House. I spent much of one term defending Durang's Christmas play against faculty charges of blasphemy (it was very funny and merely a little tasteless). When Franken came to me as a sophomore and said that he intended to become a comedian, I told him to be serious. Nadine Strossen became president of the American Civil Liberties Union. Tom Werner, of the Carsey/Werner television production team, which created *Roseanne* and *The Cosby Show*, among others, used to baby-sit for our children. And there was Tommy Lee Jones and his roommate, Al Gore.

Among my graduate student friends and junior faculty colleagues were Peretz, Wood, Thomson, and Gould, and the poets Richard Tillinghast, Frank Bidart, and Lloyd Schwartz, who won the Pulitzer Prize for music criticism in 1994, Max Byrd, a professor at the University of California at Davis and the author of rich, elegant novels on the lives of Thomas Jefferson and Andrew Jackson, Kevin

Starr, author of the remarkable history *Americans and the California Dream* and now chief librarian of California, Caroline Bynum, a professor of history at Columbia, who won a MacArthur grant, and Arvin Brown, the longtime director of the Long Wharf Theater in New Haven, Connecticut, along with a number of the country's finer and more imaginative scholars, such as Robert Ferguson of Columbia, William Alexander of the University of Michigan, John Paul Russo of Rutgers, and freelance critic Alan Weinblatt. These were only some of the ones who "made it." All were assured that the world awaited their entrance. One of the most touching books produced every five years is the *Class Book*, consisting of entries by graduates who tell what their lives have been like since commencement. When a "failure" steps forward bravely to confess that "nothing has gone the way I had hoped," one can hear the heart of the whole institution stop.

The attitude nurtured genius, arrogance, and a considerable amount of loneliness. Even today, when I walk through the Yard in which I stood twenty-seven years ago, I always feel a low, sad chord playing inside me, as if bowed by Yo Yo Ma (class of 1976), and the season is always winter. A few years ago, Ginny took a picture of me with Carl (class of 1988) when he was a senior, walking side by side from the very spot where I stood in front of Sever Hall on April 9, 1969. The shot is taken from the rear — two generations heading in the direction of University Hall. I gulp every time I look at it.

William James called Harvard "a nursery for independent and lonely thinkers," linking two not necessarily companionable conditions. James Bryant Conant (1934–53), who was succeeded by Pusey as president, said in 1936: "Harvard was founded by dissenters. Heresy has long been in the air. We are proud of the freedom which has made this possible even when we most dislike some particular form of heresy we may encounter." The sociologist David Riesman said that Harvard favored the "inner-directed" mind. Van Wyck Brooks wrote of Harvard's tolerance of exceptionality and eccentricity — more a wish than a fact as applied to the late 1960s. The exceptional or eccentric thinkers, at least in politics, kept their mouths shut or were often shouted down. Crane Brinton, who taught history for decades and was cherished by students for being Harvard's easiest grader — in some stiff competition — praised the school's "multanimity."

All such praise was tied up with a myth about the University that it encouraged brave and independent thought, but this was rarely true. "There is a Harvard man on the wrong side of every question," boasted Harvard's long-reigning president Abbott Lawrence Lowell (1909–33), who ought to have known. It was he, as chairman of a Massachusetts commission of judges, who sentenced Sacco and Vanzetti to be executed. He also opposed Brandeis for the Supreme Court, because Brandeis was a Jew. Years later Lowell was asked if there was anything that he regretted during his long tenure. "Yes," he said.

"There was a professor we could not lure away from M.I.T."

What Harvard lauded as the independent mind was more often the freakish mind, that of the outsider who had done so remarkably well in high school as to be isolated socially by the time he got to Harvard. A freshman who was assigned to me for special instruction in composition had never been to school at all. A humorless though sweet-natured stringbean, he had been educated solely by his parents, who had trained him — for some reason that made sense to them — to be a military mastermind.

From Harvard's distanced point of view, the ideal composite student would have been a fusion of John Reed and Walter Lippmann. Both were undergraduates at the same time (class of 1910, which also included T. S. Eliot, Conrad Aiken, and Joseph Kennedy), and both used their independence, or loneliness, to greatest advantage. Reed's was wild-and-woolly independence; Lippmann's, ascetic and talmudic in the sense of scholarly. He was another Jew in hiding. Both went out from Harvard to teach the world how to think about itself, and both felt empowered, indeed inspired, by an institution whose benign but watchful neglect made them believe that they were graced with extraordinary gifts.

What Harvard did not give them, or make the slightest attempt to give them or anyone, was a world of affection; more to the point, a world in which affection had a place in intellectual life. Once in a while, one will hear the University referred to as "she," as in alma mater; but the mother that is Harvard's model dresses in black and cultivates her own garden. That Reed would end up loving too easily and promiscuously, and Lippmann, too stingily, may not be blamed on their College; but the inability to use love properly impaired lives that might have been even more distinguished had they been taught that hearts and minds are related.

Under the surface of such events as McNamara, Dow, and Paine Hall was the collision between students who felt insulted by a university and a university that felt insulted by a particular generation of students. Each had assumed a reservoir of familial devotion, and there was none to draw on. They arrived at University Hall together, and the inevitable happened.

CHAPTER 7

THE COMMITTEE OF FIFTEEN held its first meeting on the evening of April 18, in Alan Heimert's Master's Residence in Eliot House. The drapes were drawn to prevent students from peering in. *Crimson* reporters waited outside for news — something they rarely received. Heimert was selected as committee spokesman, and he almost never spoke. He was a large man, not tall but solid, with a huge head and a smoky, blustery voice, which he often used to conceal a sentimental streak and an unswerving love of his students. He had grown up in working-class Chicago with a reverence for learning, and like other faculty members from working-class backgrounds, for whom Harvard meant a life of books, he was devoted to the University, perhaps too much. A scholar of American religion, his was Harvard.

Everyone seemed to sense that whatever the committee decided was going to provide the framework for all that had happened and was going to happen at Harvard that spring: the fate of the students who were involved in the takeover; the assessment of blame or praise due the administration, and Pusey in particular; the setting of events in an historical narrative that would, by its existence, provide judgment and order; and the attempted statement or restatement of the definition of university life, including rules of civil disobedience, that would be acceptable to the great majority of teachers and students. If this multiple assignment proved overwhelming, there was at least one part of it that could be achieved: the disciplining of the students. That in itself would provide a statement of order and, in the long run, would reestablish the University as the enforcer of order.

Each of the tasks was given to a separate subcommittee; this turned out to be a useful division in a number of ways. As long as the history of the causes was kept apart from the recommendation for structural change, and those two assignments were kept apart from the disciplinary decisions, it would be impossible to confuse finding fault with the University with the punishment of the students. That is, if the committee yoked its several functions under one report, the disapproval of the bust or conceivably the opposition to the war could serve as an extenuating circumstance for shoving a dean down the University Hall steps. Whatever was wrong with Harvard, as with America, was kept as a separate issue from the behavior of the people in the occupation.

John Dunlop saw clearly from the start that the disciplining of the students was the only thing that really counted; so, at our first meeting, when our three-part responsibility for discipline, history, and administrative recommendations was reiterated, Dunlop headed straight for the subcommittee, or "working group," on discipline. He was followed immediately by Jim Wilson, by Milton Katz, who became our guide on legal matters, and moments later by me. I may not have known much about university politics or about how committees operated, but I did have a sense of where the action would be. From the second I laid eyes on Dunlop, I knew that he had his own definite view of how to get Harvard back to normal. Throw out the student radicals and you'll show everyone who is in charge; that is what he understood. So did Wilson, who had the most comprehensive understanding of how what was happening at Harvard fit into American political life and social policy. What I understood, or gathered at that first meeting, was simply that I had been elected by the liberal wing of the faculty to keep an eye on these two formidable birds and perhaps to function as a countervailing force. Where they went, I went.

Along with Heimert, whom I already knew from the English department, Dunlop, Wilson, and Katz were the most forceful personalities on the committee. Hoffmann, too, had a quiet and supple power. As a child, he had been smuggled out of Nazi Germany into France during the war, and he still spoke with a French accent. He carried himself with a deferential stoop, and he had wit and a gentle disposition, but it was difficult to determine how passionately he felt about anything, and his views seemed to change depending on the mood, the day, or the person with whom he was speaking.

Holton, for all his devious energy, was a transparent operator, who had what the kids today call an attitude, but who understood very little about politics, policy, or the students. He had dark hair and small features, and bore the look of a man who harbored a secret in which no one else was interested. But he never stopped maneuvering for something or other; he would have thrived in the Soviet Union as an *apparatchik*. "How I detested him," Henry Rosovsky told me, amused at the recollection. He drove more open and direct people like Dunlop, Katz, Wilson, and Heimert up the wall.

Katz was absolutely straightforward. He was a man of high principles and a deep sense of fair play. He was wiry and looked tightly wound, but he had the kind of care-taker's soul that looks out for others; he often protected the committee from itself. He spoke with excessive preci-sion, articulating every syllable of a word, as if to ensure that the letter, like the letter of the law, would be under-stood perfectly. He was also personally brave, and he proved it at a public meeting in Mem church two months later when we had finished our work.

Ben Schwartz, the historian, was a thoughtful, humble man, roundish and usually wearing a soft smile. He looked like the stereotypical wise old men in movies.

Don Anderson, the mathematician, was tall, heavy, and a bit of a stiff, though pleasant. He spoke very little, and his face was pale, blank, and malleable. He was elected by the conservative wing of the faculty as a counterweight to me.

John Edsall, the biologist, a white-haired gray eminence, also said very little, though he probably listened more carefully than most of us.

Renée Chotiner, one of the undergraduate members, was very bright, and beautiful in the way that the actress Debra Winger is beautiful. Her radical sympathies were burdened by the fact that her uncle, Murray Chotiner, was one of Nixon's "dirty tricks" advisers.

John Fernandez felt torn, being the only black person on the committee. He leaned more to the left than Keith MacAdam or John Read. MacAdam had bright-red hair and was serious and scrupulous. Read was All-American delightful, and like Fernandez, with whom he developed a friendship, he was large and physically strong. A body builder, he wore weights around his waist to the meetings.

Bob Blumenthal, a senior, was the loosest committee member, slim, talkative, and clownish. During an especially heated debate on discipline, he proposed that we lighten up and throw a costume party, with everyone dressed as his or her favorite form of punishment.

All the members were interesting in their ways. But Wilson and Dunlop were intriguing. They and I had opposite views about the students, but I liked both of them as people. And, as it turned out, the three of us had quite similar views about the value of the University, which may be why we continue to get along well today. At the time I joined the subcommittee on discipline, however, they eyed me with deep suspicion.

Wilson was a handsome man, dashing for a Harvard professor, who had written a prophetic book called *Negro Politics* and drove fast cars. He was very orderly and self-disciplined and, though not a natural athlete, took up sports with scholarly diligence. He was great fun to work with, especially when we disagreed — very smart and quick-witted and conservative, but in that lapsed-liberal way that a lot of Catholic intellectuals, like Pat Moynihan, are or have become. He was calmly determined to beat down the radical students, and his only error was that he showed it. His evident sense of purpose put off the more moderate members of the committee, and he indicated no interest in behaving diplomatically.

John Dunlop, on the other hand, was more clever, more roundabout, and he appeared to be more flexible, which was not the case. He was neither a handsome nor an un-handsome man; neither tall nor short; fat nor thin. Indeed, he seemed to have willed the creation of a physical appear-ance that defied description and rendered him unnotice-able. He never changed his basic uniform, which consisted of a bow tie, a blue blazer, and gray slacks. His sparse black hair was slicked back. He spoke in a raspy, plaintive voice that betrayed no particular emotion. He moved like an old athlete who was trained to be careful with his body, until the moment he had use of it. In fact, he had played on the

Berkeley tennis team under Don Budge. This was known about him, though he never mentioned it or showed any interest in sports or anything other than the committee's work.

He was devoted to the art of negotiation, for which he was naturally well suited. In the fall of 1968, Arthur Goldberg, who had been secretary of labor and a Supreme Court justice before President Johnson conned him into becoming U.N. ambassador, was invited to talk at Sanders Theatre in Memorial Hall. The *Crimson* had run protests against Goldberg's speaking because of his connection with Johnson, and Franklin Ford had asked Dunlop to preside. "I spent a week interviewing every conceivable organization and interest, and arranging practice times for Arthur to talk, responses by designated people, and times for questions from related representatives," he told me. "Fortunately, the event went off without trouble. But elements in the community were seething."

Of course, fortune had little to do with it; that was the way Dunlop worked. He was on everybody's side and on nobody's side. "Travel by night, work by day" was one of his mottoes. He was indefatigable. He always said that his true gift as a negotiator was behind him; he had a hard, strong ass, and he could outsit other negotiating parties in labor disputes. Once, when we were walking together in the Yard, I mentioned a news item about a manned flight to Mars. He smiled and exulted: "More worlds to negotiate!"

He was also fond of putting on country-boy airs. If I used a phrase like *seriatim* in a sentence, or even a *status quo* or an *ad infinitum,* he would scratch his head and ask: "That's Latin, ain't it?"

Had Dunlop been an unprincipled man, he would have been one of the more dangerous people in the world. But along with his cleverness and his canniness, he had a Presbyterian sense of decency. (His parents had been missionaries in Asia.) He could, on occasion, talk like a gang boss. Of a left-wing assistant professor, he once cried out in the Faculty Club, "I'll have him by the *balls!*" Yet if he bent the rules from time to time, he never broke them, not that I saw, and I watched him carefully. And he could be helpful and sympathetic even to his antagonists. The farthest left-wing and out-of-control member of the faculty in those years was Hilary Putnam, a wild-looking philosophy professor. No faculty meeting reached adjournment without Putnam railing against the immoral war, the immoral Harvard, and his immoral colleagues. Yet when those years were over, and Hilary had changed his mind, his attire, and his politics, and he sought to recoup his reputation, he asked the help of Dunlop, who gave it readily.

When I volunteered to join the subcommittee on discipline, I saw Wilson wince, but Dunlop smiled and looked as friendly as any wolf about to greet his rabbit guest. Wilson sought to beat me down, Dunlop to co-opt me, and both succeeded a little. They wanted most if not all of the students who had participated in the takeover expelled; I wanted the expulsion only of those who had laid hands on the deans. That difference would turn into the committee's main argument.

Meanwhile, at the first meeting, we had to decide how to decide, and open hearings were agreed upon. The 135 students who had been identified as having been in University Hall would be called before a tribunal of the committee, which consisted of Dunlop, Wilson, Katz, and myself and two of the student members, Fernandez and Read. The accused were to appear one by one and explain their actions. Someone asked: "What if they don't show up?" Holton declared that anyone who refused to participate in our procedures should be expelled automatically. It was pointed out to him that students had a right not to participate. Heimert remarked to me that it would have been like Holton to first propose such a measure, and then to vote against it.

On April 30, the *Crimson* ran a piece explaining how the three working groups would proceed, but there was interest only in the disciplinary decisions. Interest intensified on May 2, when District Court Judge Viola ruled that 170 students who were arrested in University Hall at the moment of the bust were guilty of criminal trespass. A graduate student in mathematics, Carl D. Offner, was sentenced by Viola to a year in the House of Correction for assaulting Dean Watson in the takeover. The Committee of Fifteen's hearings got under way on May 4.

The identified students did, as promised, refuse to show up at the hearings. They said that they did not recognize the "legitimacy" of the Committee of Fifteen. "We had done nothing to apologize for," said Kazin, "and we were not going to apologize."

Nonetheless, schedules were drawn up containing the names of students who were to appear at each session daily, and though no one came, hearings were held every day anyway, on the tenth floor of Holyoke Center, a 1960s tower on Massachusetts Avenue across from the kiosk in the Square. It was all very eerie and surrealistic. A classroom was used for the not-attended hearings. Committee members would sit behind a long table looking at the empty chairs before us. Deans Glimp, Epps, and Watson and other deans were the only witnesses to appear.

There were attempts to disrupt the hearings. SDS mounted a protest of two hundred students the first day. A wire gate was set up at the rear stairs between the ninth and tenth floors, and student protesters screamed obscenities in the stairwell and rattled the gate. Wilson read them a prepared statement, telling them to scram. Once or twice things might have gotten violent, but they never did. The muscular presence of Read and Fernandez intimidated the protesters. For some reason, Hoffmann was terrified that the students might attack him physically, and he expressed his fear to me. But nothing ever happened worse than the shouting and the banging.

The hearings went on for five weeks, and about once a

week the committee as a whole would reconvene to report on the progress of each subcommittee. The history committee went about its task of preparing a narrative; the governance subcommittee met a lot but produced little; and our disciplinary subcommittee seemed to be producing no results whatever, though lots of notes were taken on the deans' testimonies. By determining who shoved and did not shove, we were beginning to distinguish degrees of culpability.

It was also agreed that the committee should produce a Resolution on Rights and Responsibilities as the centerpiece of its report to the faculty. It fell to me to draft the resolution, but by the time it was presented, many other writers and editors had weighed in. The purpose of such a resolution was to codify rules of behavior pertaining to political protests in the future. It was both a tricky and a thankless assignment. The more detailed the code, the more certain people, both liberal and conservative, would want precise instructions. If the resolution proved too loose and hortatory, there would be too many loopholes. Still, it was agreed that the University needed something in print to cover situations like the one we were going through — some statement of conduct that students and faculty could join hands around. A happy community agreement never materialized, but the resolution proved a necessary exercise when the committee had to justify its disciplinary decisions.

Sometimes the whole committee would meet with

groups of students in the Houses who would ask us questions ranging from the sincere to the hostile. At one such evening meeting in a Radcliffe House, SDS students burst in and surrounded Jim Wilson. They accused him of everything from subverting the education of Harvard students to belonging to the CIA and starting the Vietnam war. The more articulate of them challenged his "outdated" liberal politics. Others merely taunted him. He stood his ground. The words *Nazi* and *fascist* were used freely, as they were generally in other demonstrations and confrontations. He was smarter than most of them, more self-confident than all, and much more experienced; he knew how and when to argue. The SDS students were enraged that he could beat them in a public debate, with them shouting, nearly spitting in his face, and him sounding as cool as he did giving a lecture.

We met and we met again, and again, in the mornings, in the afternoons, in the evenings. On May 23, we sent "findings of fact" to the students who had failed to appear at the hearings. These listed specific charges ranging from manhandling the deans to merely being present in the occupied building and provided opportunities to appeal. No one did. A petition bearing over two thousand signatures was presented to the committee demanding that no students be expelled or suspended. On May 28, the committee announced that it would present its decisions at a faculty meeting on June 9.

The strike, meanwhile, which was postponed once the

faculty had taken its vote reiterating its opposition to ROTC, never resumed in force, though there were die-hard students who maintained it. It had been a haphazard strike at best. Most teachers, while supporting the students and abhorring the bust, still felt that they would be neglecting their duty if they failed to continue to hold classes.

Harry Levin had been one of those who elected to teach his classes in the Yard outside the classroom. Late one morning, I watched him from a distance. He might have been a haughty terror, as Berryman had suggested at that poetry reading. And I knew that he could be a stuffy and manipulative force in the English department. But sitting on the grass in his dark-blue pinstripe three-piece suit, with his students sitting before him, Harry looked noble.

Bill Alfred told his class in Anglo-Saxon poetry: "You can't strike. You *are* the University. You can't strike against yourselves." He said: "They looked at me as if I were cracked."

Alfred recalled: "During one of my classes, a girl suddenly burst into the room and said, 'I demand equal time to talk about the issues.' And I said to her: 'You may have five minutes. And then we're going back to work.' But she wanted to talk much longer. And one of my students, Joanne Dempsey, stood up and began to recite from *Beowulf*. Then all the students joined her. They drowned out the girl protester, and she left."

Alfred's house was a refuge not only for students who were frightened by the disruptions, but also for those who were bored with classes and who sought the companionship of one of the rarest and best-hearted people on the Harvard faculty, or anywhere. He was a lay priest at St. Paul's, the local Catholic church; he wore a ring to indicate that he was wedded to the church. He never married, but his family was every waif at Harvard, which included street kids and disaffected students equally. He still spoke with a whispery Brooklyn accent, like a Eugene O'Neill character in a bar, had a beak nose and lidded eyes, and he dressed with the three-piece elegance of a blue-collar father suiting up for Sunday mass. He had no pretenses, no airs. So modest had he been about his hit off-Broadway play, *Hogan's Goat*, that he had kept it hidden in a drawer for years, until Robert Lowell snatched it and showed it to Wynn Handman, the director of New York's American Place Theater.

Faye Dunaway, who got her start in *Hogan's Goat*, was one of the people a wide-eyed student would find at Alfred's house, though that was not my luck. I did stumble, literally, into Bernard Malamud and Lowell one day when I was a student. I had come over in the late afternoon, and, as usual, Alfred had poured me a bourbon the size of the Ritz. One shot, and I was teetering on my chair. Then Malamud and Lowell walked in, talking about Ralph Ellison. I stood up as Alfred introduced me to Malamud, and I fell into his arms.

Lillian Hellman was there another time. I heard her say to Alfred: "Don't forget, a crazy person is crazy all the time." The implication of her remark was that one ought not to be lulled into mistaking a crazy person's occasional lucid moments for anything other than a lapse. It was one of those things one hears in one's youth and makes use of later on.

That spring, Alfred's house became more of a refuge than ever. My friend Richard Tillinghast was there one time, and the three of us got looped. Tillinghast stood up and announced that he had the solution to ending the warfare. Playing Paul Henreid in *Casablanca*, he began to sing "The Marseillaise" at the top of his lungs. Alfred and I joined in. Peace was at hand.

Another day, Alfred and I were drinking lemonade in his tiny backyard with Peter Taylor, the novelist and short story writer, who had come to visit him. A group of students marched by outside the fence shouting some slogan. By now that was a common event to Alfred and me, who blithely went on chatting. But the gentlemanly Southerner Taylor looked horrified and alarmed, as if he had blundered upon a madhouse.

The two faculty caucuses continued to meet, each inventing some weird Kremlinology of the moment and ridiculing and plotting against the other caucus. The government department's Michael Walzer was elected as the leader of our Liberal Caucus, which was called the Radical Caucus by the Conservative Caucus, which called itself the

Moderate Caucus. It is hard to say what the grounds were that divided the caucuses. Some few members of the conservative-moderates believed that the war in Vietnam was a moral crusade, but most did not. The main dividing line existed between those who had sympathy for the students as students and those who did not, and between those who had approved of the bust and those who did not. Most scientists, physicists especially, for some reason, tended to side with the liberals. Most humanists leaned toward the conservatives. The social scientists seemed split down the middle.

Kelleher shared the dim humanist view of at least some of the more vocal scientists. He recalled: "From the time when the three-a-week faculty meetings began, the same dozen or so orators dominated the proceedings, endlessly informing us that since the students had given us their trust, and since the students were so right, it was our bounden duty to give in to their every demand, negotiable (if there were such) or nonnegotiable. The rest of us sat silent and fuming, thinking what all this revealed about a faculty I think most of us had romantically overestimated. It wasn't until a few others began organizing a conservative opposition that we began to realize that we were not a small and scattered sect, but that came later." He added: "Meanwhile we listened, or tried not to listen, to [biologist] George Wald." Wald's work on the eye had won the Nobel Prize. "I must admit," said Kelleher, "that he taught me some significant things, chief among them

The SDS flag flies over Harvard Yard after the seizure of University Hall.
(COURTESY MARK SILBER)

Assistant Dean Archie Epps is forced down a flight of stairs in University Hall.
(COURTESY UPI/BETTMANN)

Students protest SDS by burning an effigy of an SDS member.
(COURTESY TIMOTHY CARLSON/BETTMANN)

Dean Franklin Ford surrounded on steps of Widener Library as he orders occupiers of University Hall to leave the building.
(COURTESY TED POLUMBAUM/ LIFE MAGAZINE © TIME INC.)

One student punches another, who tried to prevent him from removing a cross from a mock graveyard in front of University Hall. The graveyard was a protest against the Vietnam War.
(COURTESY ASSOCIATED PRESS)

A student in the Faculty Room during the occupation of University Hall.
(COURTESY TIMOTHY CARLSON)

Police massed on the steps of University Hall, evicting student occupiers.
(COURTESY UPI / CORBIS-BETTMANN)

A youth hauled out of University Hall by the police.
(COURTESY ASSOCIATED PRESS)

Police in the Yard after clearing University Hall. (COURTESY THOMAS R. ITTELSON)

The Faculty Room in University Hall after occupiers had been removed from the building. (COURTESY THOMAS R. ITTELSON)

Angry students gather in
Memorial Church
in response to the police "bust."
(COURTESY MARK SILBER)

Dean of the College Fred Glimp
defends use of police to
a group of freshmen.
(COURTESY TED POLUMBAUM/
LIFE MAGAZINE © TIME INC.)

Students protest at President Nathan Pusey's house. (COURTESY MARK SILBER)

An editorial cartoon in the BOSTON HERALD TRAVELER.

A mock graveyard in the Yard protests ROTC and the Vietnam War.

Protesting students in Harvard Stadium vote on the strike.

Two alumni from a different era at commencement.

President Nathan M. Pusey.
(COURTESY FABIAN BACHRACH)

Dean of the Faculty Franklin Ford.
(COURTESY HARVARD NEWS OFFICE)

Dean of the College Fred Glimp.

Professor of English William Alfred.

Professor of economics and later
Dean of the Faculty, John Dunlop.

Professor of government Stanley Hoffmann.

Professor of law Archibald Cox.
(COURTESY W. E. TOBEY/HARVARD NEWS OFFICE)

Professor of government and leader
of the liberal caucus, Michael Walzer.
(COURTESY W. E. TOBEY/HARVARD NEWS OFFICE)

Professor of economics
Alexander Gerschenkron.
(COURTESY W. E. TOBEY/HARVARD NEWS OFFICE)

Master of Eliot House and
professor of English, Alan E. Heimert.
(COURTESY W. E. TOBEY/HARVARD NEWS OFFICE)

Professor of government James Q. Wilson.
(COURTESY HARVARD NEWS OFFICE)

Dean of the Law School
and later University President, Derek C. Bok.
(COURTESY W. E. TOBEY/HARVARD NEWS OFFICE)

Assistant professor of government Martin Peretz.
(COURTESY MARTIN PERETZ)

Professor of economics and chair of the committee on Afro-American studies, Henry Rosovsky.
(COURTESY W. E. TOBEY/HARVARD NEWS OFFICE)

The author as assistant professor of English and Master of Dunster House, with his wife, Ginny, and son, Carl.

what a dangerous thing a Nobel Prize is, for if a man has any tendency toward misplaced omniscience, getting the prize brings it out in spades. Obviously I wasn't the only one who felt that. There was the guy from the government department — I never knew his name — who said, 'Every time that son of a bitch sits down I have an almost uncontrollable urge to leap to my feet and deliver a lecture on the physiology of the eye.'"

The more prominent scientists made more noise than sense. Jim Watson declared at one faculty meeting that ROTC "insults" the faculty and the student body. "Also," he asked, "from the military point of view, is it doing any good? I do not think it is protecting us from either the Red or Yellow Menace."

At the time I guessed that the humanists were more conservative because they had a deeper respect for history; and that the scientists were more liberal because they worked in the present and the future, and liked to stir the pot. They lived to experiment, which meant that the status quo (i.e., institutions) had no sanctity for them. At our Liberal Caucus meetings Jim Watson and biologist Mark Ptashne clearly loved to keep tempers boiling to see what would cook. And even Holton, who was more on the fringes of science as a historian, might have been driven to trouble the waters as much by professional bent as by his character. To a large degree, though, each group was made up of people who simply did not like some people in the other group.

Many faculty members were worn down or out by the hysteria and by the pace. "The students panicked us," said Bill Alfred. "They were like stampeding animals — and one thing going on after another." Like many others, Alfred adored Erik Erikson, the great social psychologist, who was very old and patriarchal and whose cloud of white hair seemed to be lit from the inside. Alfred told me: "At faculty meetings I used to look over to see how Erik was voting, because I was so confused. I think a lot of people did. And then, you know, he began not to vote."

Professor of government Samuel Beer, the most admired liberal on the faculty and a longtime hero to undergraduates, said that he felt about the students "the way I do about Germans. There are some good Germans. Some of my best friends are students. But when I hear the word *student* I pull back reflexively."

One sentimental moment, both touching and out of place because of its decency, occurred at a faculty meeting when classicist Herbert Bloch, a German Jew, proposed that the University flag be hung on the stage of the Loeb Drama Center while we were meeting. Bloch, who was tall, aristocratic, and gentle, and who still spoke with a German accent, cited the symbolic solace that he felt was offered by the flag in the "sober anonymity" of the Drama Center.

"I have always been particularly proud of the 'Veritas' emblem," he said. "The more so as I come from a part of Europe where then the lie was the main weapon of propaganda, where leaders could shamelessly proclaim as their principles that the bigger the lie, the more readily it would be accepted, and that a lie repeated often enough would eventually become belief. Not so many years ago, attempts were made to introduce these tenets into our life. I — and I *know* I am not alone — still feel profound gratitude to all at the helm of Harvard then, who lived up to our ancient 'Veritas' motto and saved the University.

"Now we are again in a crisis. As I look around me and recognize the many familiar faces, as I remember the countless rewarding conversations I have had in the last thirty years with many of you in fields distant from my own, I wish to confess the awe and admiration I have felt and feel now for this faculty. To preserve its distinction must be one of the chief goals of our coming deliberations. Let us not forget our sense of history lest we lose our sense of destiny, and let us place the emblem of the University before us here to deepen that feeling of commitment which all of us share."

The motion was carried without discussion by a voice vote. Then the faculty returned to the business as usual of sniping at one another.

European-born faculty had not always sided with the administration. In the late 1950s, the federal government was offering National Defense Education Act (NDEA) grants for graduate students to hasten the country's closing of the *Sputnik*-inspired "missile gap" with the Soviet Union. Those NDEA grants included loyalty oaths; if the recipient did not sign, he would not get a grant. Like other universities, Harvard, when it administered those grants, gave tacit sanction to the loyalty oaths. At a faculty meeting in 1957, members protested. McGeorge Bundy, then Dean of the Faculty of Arts and Sciences who later was appointed special assistant for national security affairs by President Kennedy, explained that the University was playing no part in the oath-taking. It was merely sending the signed oaths back to Washington. "We're simply licking the stamps," Bundy told the faculty. Renato Poggioli, the renowned Italian scholar, rose to reply in his broken English. "Mr. Dean," he said. "I have spent much of my life in Fascista Italy. And in Fascista Italy, you learna one thing. First you licka the stamps. Then you licka something else."

Many professors were alarmed at this time, too, that the government was sticking its nose into University business. On April 27, James Reston, who had been outraged by the University Hall attack, wrote in the *New York Times:* "Concessions made by the faculties and administrations at [places like] Harvard to the use of force by campus militants have convinced officials here [in Washington] that justice is too serious a business to be left to university teachers and officials who submit to the use and threat of force." On May 28, Dean Elder of the Graduate School of Arts and Sciences was subpoenaed by the Senate Subcommittee on Investigations of the Committee on Government Operations, chaired by Senator John L. McClellen (D-Ark.), to appear and present the records of twenty-one students who were in SDS or who were caught in the University Hall occupation. He said that he did not cooperate. On May 30, the *Crimson* reported that Harvard administrators responding to another subpoena sent the Senate Subcommittee the names of thirty-two students involved in University Hall who were receiving federal aid. This was later denied by the administration.

It was difficult to tell how serious the government was in pursuing student protesters, but I took the impression that if the University had encouraged interference, there were many people in and out of the Nixon administration who would have been glad to send them straight to Vietnam. The Senior Tutors agreed among ourselves that we would not respond to any outside requests for students' names. One afternoon, two tall, smiling FBI agents came to my office to ask about certain Dunster House students. They were grimly displeased to be turned away.

One event, or pseudo-event, did bring the faculty caucuses together briefly. Someone had learned that the SDS had planned to attack Widener Library, perhaps to destroy the books. I received a call from Merle Fainsod, the Harvard Librarian, late one afternoon. Merle said that he was phoning a number of faculty members to ask if they would stand with him in the library and ward off the attackers.

We gathered, about twenty-five of us liberals and conservatives, at eleven that night, when the library was closed, greeted one another solemnly, and milled about the reading room. Most of the people there were older professors, like Herschel Baker, an elegant Texan and a much-admired Elizabethan scholar, who used to pin any student to the door who dared to try to leave his lecture before the bell — "Young man, ah haven't finished" — and the historians Donald Fleming and Oscar Handlin. Oscar was one of the great minds and spirits at Harvard. His indispensable work on turn-of-the-century immigrants had its roots in his own life, and I believe that he associated one's ability to rise in the University with the ability to raise one's status in America. The students' rebellion enraged and pained him. Every one of us was concerned that the rumors of an attack would turn out to be true, but no one more than Oscar. I could only guess what was going through his mind as he contemplated the idea of young, organized idealogues mounting an assault on books.

But the rumor was not true. We waited a few hours and then dispersed, to return on two more nights. I suppose that our vigils looked foolish and alarmist to some people, and that students, learning of them, laughed that we would actually think they were capable of destroying one of the great centers of learning in the world. Perhaps it was an overreaction, but I did not believe so at the time, and I knew that the more radical students were perfectly capable of storming Widener. After University Hall and the bust, there was reason to think that anything could happen at Harvard.

Foolish or not, there was something good and civilized about those nights. In retrospect, if the so-called left- and right-wing members of the faculty had taken that symbolic opportunity to discuss beliefs they held in common, such as the value of Widener Library, some of the bitterness among the faculty in future years might have dissipated.

So frequent were strange and wild events during those weeks that the Widener nights were hardly noted. There were several fistfights in the Houses between SDS members and more conservative students, athletes in particular. SDS and Progressive Labor members got into fights as well. The two groups were distinguishable on sight; Progressive Labor members wore ties because they did not want to offend the working class.

Shouting matches in the halls were normal. The driver of a Harvard laundry truck was stopped while making deliveries and dragged from the cab by some SDS students because the operation was non-union. He was chased from his truck, the truck was overturned, and dozens of bags of laundry were scattered on Flagg Street near Dunster House.

On April 22, about four hundred supporters of the SDS Eight Demands took over University Hall again, from about noon to 5 P.M. Unlike the more violent April 9 takeover, this one, termed a "mill-in," involved no ouster of the deans or invasions of files. The demonstrators entered and, where they could, engaged the administration in arguments. Business was disrupted, and the secretaries were evacuated. There was no action taken against the students. Dean of Students Watson, who had been shoved around the most on April 9, told these demonstrators: "If you want to invade the building, we obviously won't set up an armed guard to prevent it."

On May 6, a fire was set on the ground floor of the ROTC building. It did considerable damage, and arson was suspected. On May 7, the *Crimson* ran a letter signed by four members of the class of 1967. It read: "The undersigned condemn the hypocritical racist lies and slander of Patrician Pig Pusey, Faculty Flunky Ford, Patrician Punk von Stade . . . and Weenie Whizzer Watson as Mad-dog Insanity and naked aggression against the People(s)." Forty Eliot House seniors announced plans to burn their diplomas at commencement.

The *Crimson* was driving much of the faculty crazy, with what the more conservative members thought to be its incendiary leftward tilt. Looking at back issues now, it seems clear that in the letters columns, which were ample, the presentation of pro-University and anti-University views was even-handed. But the editorials were relentless in their condemnation of the bust and their support of the strike and the SDS demands. News articles, too, which are always more influential than editorials, suggested that anything the administration and the faculty did was suspect. Every move of the Committee of Fifteen was tracked like a scandal about to be disclosed.

Faculty members looking for a more objective account of events were not helped by the *Boston Globe*, either. The paper hired as its Harvard correspondent a man named

Parker Donham, who had been executive editor of the *Crimson* in 1968, had left school briefly to serve in the Eugene McCarthy presidential campaign and then returned to the College. Donham's pieces for the *Globe* were such that they might as well have appeared in the *Crimson;* indeed, he wrote a piece on "Covering Harvard" from the outside for the *Crimson,* which offered a foretaste of the advocacy journalism of the 1990s, in which he stated that "the style of journalism the administration loves may be a thing of the past." Sam Beer was so infuriated at the *Globe,* he stopped writing book reviews for them.

In his 1969 *New York Times Magazine* article, Tony Lukas wrote: "The *Crimson* today is a different paper [from when he worked on it in the 1950s]. Few of its editors have any interest in the law or daily journalism. When I asked one *Crimson* executive why he wouldn't accept a job on the *Times,* he said, 'Daily journalism describes what is. I want to describe what should be.'"

The *Crimson's* often thoughtless leanings to the left eventually produced an equally thoughtless reaction from the right. In the fall of 1969, an editorial supporting the national moratorium of October 15, which involved a work stoppage at universities to protest the war, ran with the title: "End the War: Support the NLF." The NLF was the National Liberation Front of the Vietnamese Communists. The editorial read: "The 'enemy' in Vietnam as embodied in the Provisional Revolutionary Government is fighting for national self-determination, and should be supported, not opposed." It so incensed some faculty members that they got together with *Crimson* alumni in an effort to persuade the graduate alumni board of the paper to step in and take it over. Jim Fallows, who was the *Crimson* president by that time, still fumed in recalling a meeting that he was called to by a former *Crimson* executive, Hiller Zobel (class of 1953), now a federal judge in Massachusetts, at which Zobel represented the view that the paper needed a correction of course. Zobel and several faculty members, including Handlin, Beer, and government professor Arthur Maass (the author of *Muddy Waters*, one of the first important books on the environment) later met with Lukas, Halberstam, and other *Crimson* graduate board members to ask them to exert a moderating influence on Fallows and the current editors. But Lukas and Halberstam pointed out what would have been obvious to them in less heated times. Halberstam told me: "I just said, 'It's their paper, let them make their mistakes.'" The *Crimson* opponents were sufficiently riled up, however, that they put out a flier called "Rap-Up" in the spring of 1969, which contradicted information in the *Crimson,* and in the following year some of them raised money to launch the *Harvard Independent* as a weekly competitor with the *Crimson.*

More and more, the students seemed to be becoming radicalized — not because the great majority of moderates were changing their politics, but because they were growing more silent and the SDS students were emboldened.

"Harvard Gets an Education," ran a headline in the *Old Mole:* "The battle for the Eight Demands [presented to the University when the strike was originally called] has a dual purpose and a dual impact," wrote Jon Weiner, a graduate student in government. "To win the demands and to raise the level of political understanding among students. To gain the demands will be to impair the University's ability to rule Cambridge and to hamper its efforts to supply sophisticated leadership for the army which polices the world. . . . Political discussion and political action are now the daily activity of roughly ten times as many people as the 100 to 200 who formed the SDS chapter."

There could be no question that many more students were talking politics, or at least were listening to those who did the talking. But I could tell from watching the Dunster House students alone, who along with Adams House counted more radical students than other Houses, that, while the noise level was increasing, it was no sign of the true feelings of the student body. Most students still deplored SDS and its tactics. But now they also were angry at Harvard for the bust, and they never lost their fear of, and fury against, the war. "It was Vietnam," Galbraith said. "Only and always Vietnam."

That was probably true for the majority. But the hard-core SDS students maintained a varied agenda. A twenty-page pamphlet titled "Harvard, Urban Imperialist" was remarkable for the detail in its accusations against the University's real-estate policies. The general student body could not have been less interested in that issue, nor could they have had the time or the patience to become expert in it. But they had to be affected by the growing atmosphere. With a very few and isolated exceptions, no one on the faculty or the administration was speaking up for Harvard, so the political spoils went to the group making the most noise. Nonetheless, the quietest group of Harvard students was also the largest.

The *Old Mole* kept churning out copy. One of the more noteworthy things it published was a chart called "How Harvard Rules." It drew lines of interconnection of Harvard people with corporate and political power in America, in an attempt to have readers draw the conclusion that Harvard was creating the war in Vietnam and waging a parallel war against the nation's poor. If the chart failed in that effort, it was interesting simply for indicating how far Harvard reached into national and international life. The Corporation — William Marbury, Francis Burr, Albert Nickerson, R. Keith Kane, George Bennett, and Hugh Calkins — were directors of banks, utilities, and oil companies. Overseers such as journalist Theodore White, *Newsweek* editor Osborn Elliott, and *Boston Globe* publisher W. Davis Taylor were powerful in the media. Others like David Rockefeller, Paul Nitze, and C. Douglas Dillon were national figures.

A year earlier, in the spring of 1968, I had been given a personal glimpse of Harvard's importance in world affairs. I was peripherally involved in a closed-door meeting between David Rockefeller and Lee Kuan Yew, the prime minister of Singapore. Yew and Rockefeller had scheduled the meeting in Dunster House, and as Senior Tutor, I was asked by the University Marshal, an old horse-face from another era, who was Harvard's chief of protocol, to greet Yew at Dunster House when he arrived. "Don't forget to put up the Singapore flag," he instructed me. When I told him that I did not have the Singapore flag handy, he grudgingly sent one over. He coached me in how to address the prime minister properly — "your highest excellency" or "your greatest highness," or something like that. I stood at curbside on Memorial Drive, muttering and practicing my greeting.

Yew's limousine slid up, he emerged, I started to address him: "Welcome to Harvard, your highest . . ."

"Never mind that," said the prime minister. "Get me some tea. Very hot. Very black." Then he went upstairs for his private meeting with Rockefeller.

The *Old Mole* called its chart "a detailed and definitive examination of Harvard's role in ruling the empire," and it pretty much made its case. But I was unsure if the effect of that chart was to anger and mobilize the majority of students, or to impress them. Given that many of the students were destined for the same positions that the *Old Mole* exposed and decried, with the same connections, they might have been less interested in beating the enemy than in joining them.

Rather than experiencing a revolutionary change in political thinking, most students seemed to feel a general cultural freedom from authority. They might not have been sure what to do with that freedom, but its possibilities seemed clearly better than the old order. While the strike was in force, Nicholas Gagarin, a well-liked third-year student who published a novel, *Windsong*, while still an undergraduate, and who killed himself not long after he graduated, wrote in the *Crimson:* "The carnival nature of some aspects of the strike springs from the fact that for the first time in recent years we find ourselves with some breathing room. Suddenly, we have won a victory. Suddenly we see that the cycle may not be closed, that we may not be doomed by the system to lives of corporate boredom. Suddenly we are free and we find that education is not what we have always been told it is. Suddenly everything is open."

Only a very small number of Harvard students were true-believer political or cultural radicals. They won the more quiet majority to their side, not because they were persuasive or appealing in themselves, but because authority — all forms of authority — was unappealing. What created the left-leaning majority at Harvard — and probably at other turbulent institutions — was the fact that if a choice had to be made between a boy with a bullhorn and the building behind him, the building went.

For every student who made the most of his liberation, there was at least one other who flipped out. A woman who is a magazine editor today told me with more regret than amusement that she was high on drugs that entire spring. Students would bang on the door of my Senior Tutor's residence in the middle of the night, shaking and in tears. We talked and talked. I took a couple of them over to the psychiatric services in Holyoke Center, where we sat waiting for the doctors, some of whom were no more help than anyone else. A psychiatrist greeted a student who was on the verge of a nervous breakdown: "You know, this won't get you out of exams."

One afternoon I watched a boy with a shaved head and a hard, strained face, who was dressed in a green t-shirt and jeans, wend his way through a crowd in the Yard yelling: "Fuck you! And you! And *you!*" As he passed, people followed him with their stares. Then he spun around, glowered at them, and yelled: "Fuck everybody!"

The Committee of Fifteen continued to meet, the students in the Houses continued to meet, SDS continued to meet, the Corporation met both with itself and with the Houses, and the faculty met. Every faculty meeting was huge — rancorous, silly, yet often something else. Most of these men led private, enclosed lives — scholars who had become scholars to escape or avoid the world of politics into which they were now dragged. Before that spring they would haul themselves to sleepy faculty meetings once a month and sit together quietly and comfortably, as if they had all slipped into the same heavy wool flannel suit. Now nearly everyone became an orator. The professors who had held government posts or who did a lot of work outside the University, like Galbraith, were more polished when they addressed the meetings, but people like Gerschenkron and Bloch were more affecting because they stumbled about in efforts to turn their often inchoate feelings into formalistic motions and amendments; frequently they would blunder into eloquence.

But the general atmosphere of the meetings remained tense. There was always someone ready for a fight. Pusey retained his impassive calm, except for that one exchange with Galbraith. So did Ford — until that blowup with Morton White. Shortly after White had attacked him, Ford had a minor stroke and was taken to Massachusetts General Hospital. He recovered fully, to everyone's relief, but his affliction marked the low point for many who remember that spring. When I asked Bill Alfred if that time was as bad as I thought it was, he answered simply, "Franklin's stroke."

There was a high point, for my family at least. On the very night of the first meeting of the Committee of Fifteen, Ginny went into labor with Amy. Shortly after one in the morning on April 19, I called the University Police to ask if someone could drive us to Boston Lying-In Hospital. Ginny's mother had come to stay with us to take care of Carl. The cop who drove us to the hospital was almost as petrified as I that Ginny would start to give birth in the car, and he remained very, very quiet. Amy was born at about 6:30. She looked perfect, of course. I remembered Kelleher, who had four daughters, telling me that every girl baby who is born looks up from the crib, sees her father, and thinks: "Sucker." That would be fine with me.

I had time to make sure that Ginny and our daughter were well, time to get back to Dunster to tell Carl that he had a new baby sister (he took the news manfully), and time to get over to Sever on the run to teach my class in modern poetry. I dumped my books on the desk, looked up at my students, and announced Amy's birth. Everybody clapped.

CHAPTER 8

OF ALL THE ISSUES the faculty addressed during those weeks, the one that most clearly revealed their attitudes about the students was black studies. The issue involved giving greater autonomy to the black students in shaping their own course of study. When it came to a head at one astonishing meeting, one of two things became evident: either the majority of the faculty were eager to give student protesters anything they wanted because they genuinely believed that that would help them; or they were eager to give them too much rope because they wanted the students to hang themselves. Either way, what the faculty voted in terms of black studies could not have turned out worse for the intellectual life of the students they were claiming to help.

On April 22, at a meeting in the Loeb Drama Center, a motion was presented to overturn the vote taken in February, in which the faculty approved the establishment of a Committee on Afro-American Studies, and to now create a full-fledged Afro-American Studies department. The motion also called for six students to be included along with faculty members on a committee with the responsibility of planning the design of the new department. Student members would decide which students would graduate with honors; they were to vote on tenure as well as term appointments; and they would join the executive committee of the department when it was formed. This would give a group of black students at Harvard powers that up to then had been held only by senior faculty. Junior faculty members had no vote on tenure appointments. The motion thus violated both tradition and sense.

It was also made under two threats, one of which was stupidly comical, though it was taken seriously by some members of the faculty. Professors walking into the meeting on April 22 were greeted by the sight of a black student carrying a meat cleaver. At worst this kid represented but one more element of symbolic idiocy, but there were people who claimed to believe that were the black studies department vote to go against the protesters, he would run amok, lopping off heads. As the faculty's actions soon proved, he did not need to expend the effort.

Kelleher, who called that day "the most shameful in Harvard history," recalled entering the hall with two department colleagues. One professed to be terrified by the student with the "weapon," even when the other said, "Don't be silly; he's just signifying the name of that leader — what is it? — Eldridge Cleaver."

The more articulate threat made to the faculty was delivered by an undergraduate, Leslie Griffin, who was a leader in the Association of African and Afro-American Students (A.A.A.A.S.). Griffin presented the A.A.A.A.S. demands to the faculty meeting. He told the Harvard faculty that the black students, like SDS, had had the opportunity to disrupt the University but had not seized it; he knew that the Harvard faculty would act honorably on the amendment; and finally he said, "Not to pass this resolution is a serious mistake . . . from which this University might not be able to recover."

Not only was the resolution idiotic on the face of it; it overturned the work of a committee headed by Henry Rosovsky that had produced a report that the faculty had overwhelmingly accepted only two months earlier. Rosovsky's committee had been created in the wake of the riots that followed Martin Luther King's assassination in April 1968. He was chosen for this task, not because he had any experience with black studies, but because of his good heart and balanced judgment. His family were Jewish refugees from Poland, and Henry still spoke with an Eastern European intonation. He shuffled his feet and shrugged and gestured and walked with the slight stoop of an older man. He was the Old World, but he had a sense of the needs of the new one, one of which was to attend to the lives of black students in primarily white universities.

His committee had worked on its report from May 1968 to January 1969. Though Rosovsky understood that the social life of black students needed attention, he was mainly concerned with their intellectual dignity. In a total enrollment of over three thousand graduate students in the Graduate School of Arts and Sciences, only twenty were black. Rosovsky wrote in the *American Scholar:* "It seems to me true that the social sciences and the humanities have treated the American Negro in rather offhand fashion. His literature is not commonly studied in universities and his music is welcome on the dance floor but not in the classrooms. The traditional disciplines have not provided an atmosphere in which subject matter directly related to black Americans has flourished."

His committee recommended the following: that a social center be created, that a research center be created, that graduate scholarships be offered, and that a combined undergraduate concentration in Afro-American studies be established. The committee further placed students on a personnel search committee to suggest names of teachers. It recommended that Afro-American studies be designated a faculty committee rather than a department because a committee could develop organically and with a greater chance of permanent success. History and Literature, one of Harvard's most interesting and selective concentrations, was a committee.

When the Rosovsky Committee's report was issued in January, there were conservative members of the faculty who thought its recommendations represented a capitulation to politics, but Rosovsky held his ground. In essence, he argued, what was wrong with politics? If American universities could pour tens of millions of dollars into Russian and Chinese studies in a politically inspired effort to stay ahead of the Russians and the Chinese, why should it not attend to urgent business at home?

Counterbalancing the conservatives in the faculty were a minority of black students who felt that the committee report did not go far enough. But the great majority of students and faculty expressed satisfaction with the report, and the faculty happily adopted it in February. Why was it willing to turn on its own vote in April?

I had a hint of the reason as a result of a personal involvement with black studies that began casually and then became serious and consuming. In the fall of 1968, four or five black students living in Dunster House came to me with the request that I help them study the literature of black Americans. I told them that I did not know anything about the literature, except for having read a little of Richard Wright, Ralph Ellison, and James Baldwin, and that I did not even know enough about American literature to set the works and writers in context. They said that my ignorance did not matter to them, since I at least had the skill of being able to read books critically. Besides, they knew me from the House. Two of them had played in pickup basketball games with me at the Indoor Athletic Building (IAB), Harvard's name for the gym, and because of my reputation as a bleeding heart, I was the only member of the English department whom they felt they could approach.

What had rightly discouraged and insulted them was that no course offered by the English department contained the work of a single black writer. Not even the survey course in American literature included among the modern writers worth studying Ellison, Wright, or Baldwin. The students who came to me wanted to study these writers and others under any circumstances I would provide for them. We agreed to meet in the evenings once every two weeks in the Dunster Junior Common Room to talk over the material.

Of all the teaching experiences I have had over the years, none was as enjoyable or as interesting as this. Between our biweekly meetings we would read one, perhaps two novels or autobiographies in preparation for our discussions. From the purely intellectual point of view, the experience was eye-opening for all of us. We saw not only that the writing of black authors was complex and layered and equipped with a special mythology, but that it also presented a way of seeing America that was fascinating and original. LeRoi Jones (before he changed his name to Amiri Baraka) said that the black man in America is like a person who has been kept locked in a small room of a great house by white men. When that person is let out of that room and wanders about, he knows the whole house, whereas his white jailers do not. My students and I began to feel like that black prisoner released. In the works of Paul Laurence Dunbar, James Weldon Johnson, Jean Toomer, Zora Neale Hurston, and Langston Hughes, as well as more well known writers and more recent ones such as Chester Himes, Paule Marshall, and William Melvin Kelley, we saw America through a door that was wholly new to me and mostly new to them, though some had experienced the things that we were reading about.

The course, though it offered no formal credits, got to be quite demanding. The more we read, the more we wanted to read. The group grew from an initial half dozen to over twenty-five. Students from other Houses heard about it and came to join. Most were black, but not all. We sat around a long wooden table below a dim brass chandelier. We spoke of our lives in connection with the works, but we never overdid that. This was a course in literature, like any other. We discussed plot, character, theme, style, and language. What had begun for me as mostly a social gesture, a way to make up for a deficiency in the department syllabus, soon grew into a genuine interest.

The following fall, I taught Black Fiction in America as a lecture course. *Newsweek* ran a piece on burgeoning black studies programs and courses throughout the country in which it mentioned mine. It noted that though I was white, "the black students seem to accept him. 'Rosenblatt doesn't try to come across as the sympathetic race liberal,' says one. He doesn't have to. He's talking about black fiction and he's got his stuff down cold." I surely wanted to have the material down cold, because that was the only kind of sympathy that made sense to me.

From my conversations with black students in the House, I had become aware of how tricky their lives were at Harvard. When they were not ignored they were patronized. One of the first group of students who had approached me was a senior, John Tyson — a roommate of Al Gore and Tommy Lee Jones — who was so good a defensive back, he had already received feelers from the National Football League in his junior year. But in the summer before his senior year, he had decided that he did not want to play football for Harvard. He told me that he did not want to be "a hired gladiator" for his Harvard masters, and that he wanted to devote himself to studies.

At the time I remember thinking that he was being melodramatic, but what he chose to do was his business. Then the football coach called me, begging me to intervene to get John back on the team. I realized in that phone conversation that Tyson might be right. The coach did not even pretend to care about the boy's mind or his future outside football. The reason that intellectual life was so important to black students at Harvard was that by sharing in it equally, they were participating in the main purpose of the University. By looking at its black students as athletes, or as a color quota, Harvard was telling them that they would always be peripheral to America, and the students understood this, and they wanted more.

They wanted an honest appraisal of their individual worth as well. Years after I had left Harvard, a black former Dunster House student came to me distraught that he had been turned down for a junior partnership in his law firm. "They told me I couldn't write well enough, but nobody except you told me that at Harvard." Telling a student that he had something to learn, of course, was a way of saying that he was capable of learning it, but too many teachers, at Harvard and elsewhere, either did not want to teach black students or had developed the lunatic notion that to identify someone's educational deficiency was to do injury to his pride. As the faculty vote on the black studies department would demonstrate, to lie to a student, any student, about his capabilities was to pave the way to his failure later.

The deep pleasure of that course we were taking with one another was that it was the real thing — an honest, freewheeling examination of valuable material. There was no political cheerleading in the group. Some black writers or works were judged wonderful, others were the pits. When the Rosovsky Committee presented its report in January, our group was happy. What the proposed committee was about to do for black studies on a large scale, we had been doing on a small one. I knew from firsthand experience that the majority of black students were more than content with the report. If they changed their minds in the spring, it was because they felt that the University was not acting fast enough to implement it. Indeed, Harvard was yet to make a single appointment to the field, or to get the courses lined up. A minority took advantage of a politically charged atmosphere and persuaded the majority to make extreme demands. Most of the students were simply acting out of frustration.

But the real culprits were the faculty, and it was interesting to observe how certain members revealed their true feelings and alliances in the April 22 meeting. Several who were known to be on the side of the students in other fundamental matters tried to persuade their colleagues what a bad idea this was. Like Sam Beer, with whom they were frequently at odds at this time, they were old-time liberals, who appreciated the difference between reform and destruction. There was nothing reflexive or offhand about their sympathies with the students, nor did they believe that putting students in a position to ruin an endeavor was the way to help them or the endeavor.

H. Stuart Hughes, a professor of history who was in the forefront of the antiwar movement and had run for Massachusetts senator against Teddy Kennedy (in his first race in 1962) on an antinuclear platform, rose to speak against the motion. Stuart, an amiable and self-assured man, was a grandson of the Supreme Court Justice Charles Evans Hughes. He was also a member of the Rosovsky Committee and noted that the work of that committee, once "happy and almost invariably harmonious" was not so now, "and this is a great source of grief to those of us who produced what we regarded as an important report [in January] that was accepted overwhelmingly by the faculty."

He went on: "A role for students in developing curriculum is entirely appropriate," but "a role for students in recommendations for tenure, or in deciding on degree-awarding and honors, is not appropriate."

Frank Freidel, the eminent FDR biographer, who taught one of the first two courses for credit on black studies at Harvard the following year (mine being the other), rose to say: "I do not feel that it is fair to the [black] students to develop a program in which . . . the faculty will probably not be of the best quality, because some of the best people will not come." Moreover, "the faculty who come will find themselves dependent upon student popularity," and "the students will find themselves having to obtain the approval of their peers in order to receive their degrees."

Then the opposition voices in favor of the motion arose one after the other. Jim Watson, who as far as I knew had no connection with black studies or with many black students, said: "I would like to speak in favor of the proposal, largely because I believe in trusting the young. And thinking of my own career — when I was a student, when Francis [Crick] and I were doing my work, and I should point out that Francis didn't have a Ph.D. — we could have picked a much better faculty for Harvard University than I think the faculty at that time could have. And I say this not against the faculty as such, but when you're doing something new, the older people are not doing something new. This group of students wants to do something new. Let them do it. I think they will do it better than men of forty, and if it is to be done well it's going to be done by people under the age of twenty-five. I don't think we should delude ourselves into thinking that people above the age of twenty-five will have the guts to do it."

Others followed him, spouting the same general line. This was the time for new thinking, they said. Young people deserved this chance to rule their own lives. Black studies was different from other studies, special, unique. And so on. I could not believe what I was hearing. Why were people who claimed to be devoted to academic excellence carelessly scuttling a new program before it started? And in the name of sensitivity?

Joel Porte, an associate professor of American literature, now joined the bandwagon of support. Porte was known as a whiny and gossipy figure in the English department; one colleague called him Portnoy. Once in his Quincy House office, he had expressed to me his personal fear of the protesting black students. When I heard him speak for the motion, I felt certain that some destructive motive underlay this sudden faculty reversal.

He said: "I think we're entering a period when students in general will have to be brought into decisions affecting curriculum and appointments. I believe this is the appropriate — indeed the imperative — time to make this departure from past procedure. It will represent a step forward, I think, not only for the black community, but for Harvard at large. I am deeply impressed by the good faith and hard work of the students in the Association of African and Afro-American Students. Their desire to work constructively in the formation of a new and necessary program deserves respect and, I firmly believe, strong support."

The vote was taken. It passed by a large number. Defeated faculty members were numb.

Kelleher had always gauged the way he voted by watching Marty Peretz and then voting the opposite way. But on this motion, Peretz would have nothing to do with student sympathies; he knew what was at stake.

"Look!" a colleague once said to Kelleher as a vote was taken. "Peretz has deserted us! He's on our side!"

After the April 22 meeting, Holton, Hoffmann, and three other professors who had supported the motion added an insult to intelligence to the injury of the vote in a letter to the *New York Times*. The paper had severely criticized the faculty turnaround. The letter stated, in a hilarious equivocation and evasion of fact, that giving students a vote on tenure "does not give them power to appoint tenure professors. By long-standing Harvard practice, tenure appointments to the Faculty of Arts and Sciences are made by the President and Fellows only after detailed consideration and approval by an *ad hoc* committee to study the merits of each proposed tenure appointee." The fact was that *ad hoc* committees almost never turned down faculty recommendations and would be highly unlikely to do so when black students were on the committee making the recommendations.

Rosovsky said that the faculty passed the motion out of panic. But I felt that while some few may have panicked, others were motivated by moral carelessness. They were perfectly willing to throw black studies into chaos because the subject did not affect them. They could not care less what happened to black studies at Harvard. Certainly, most of the senior members of the English department treated my interest in the subject contemptuously. I could tell this from the unctuous way they congratulated me for taking the subject on. And there was the fact, which my first black students discovered, of the total absence of black literature in department offerings. The course that the students and I created was one in which artistic and intellectual respectability were properly accorded black writers. Similar rump courses, such as one in history taught by my friend Peter Wood, were the only ones to deal with the black American experience. Until it became clear that this sort of ghetto treatment of a huge and important population was intolerable, those little informal courses were it.

I believe that many, if not the majority, of the faculty acted as they did simply because, perhaps unconsciously, they wanted the black students to isolate themselves even further than they were already. They wanted the entire issue out of the way. In a darker sense, they were enacting the sort of triage that policemen practice when they refuse to patrol violent black inner-city neighborhoods. They say, in effect, "Let them kill themselves." The Harvard faculty who voted to allow undergraduates to make decisions about tenure and other departmental matters that were far beyond their experience or capabilities were also saying, "Let them kill themselves."

So they did. The Afro-American Studies department was created as a result of the April 22 vote. The student-faculty committees proceeded to invite the most distinguished black scholars in the country to join it. None would, as Freidel had rightly predicted. John Hope Franklin, the great University of Chicago historian, turned down the proffered chairmanship of the department flat. Others did as well. Ordinarily, an invitation to become a permanent member of the Harvard faculty was accepted eagerly, but no self-respecting scholar was going to rush to a department run by students.

The only person that the committee could find to accept the offer was Ewart Guinier, the father of the ill-fated friend of the Clintons Lani Guinier (class of 1971). Guinier had no academic experience whatever; he had been a labor leader. He was affable, glad to take the job, and thoroughly unsuited for it. Michael Walzer and Marty Peretz went to Dunlop to urge him to support a distinguished scholar, Stuart Hall, a Jamaican Englishman, for department chairman. But for some reason, Dunlop supported Guinier.

Others hired were also inept. Under Guinier the Afro-American Studies department became a slum. Students flocked to it at the start, full of enthusiasm for the new venture. But soon they saw that they were getting little in return, and with each successive year, the number of concentrators dwindled. At last, in early 1973, the faculty eliminated the special role of students in the department. This occurred when Dunlop was Dean of the Faculty. But not until Guinier retired and Orlando Patterson, a respected sociologist from Columbia, replaced him did the department begin to come into its own. That took ten years.

During those years a ruinous black nationalism set in at Harvard and other universities that has not gone away yet. Even before the spring of 1969, black students were beginning to sit only with one another in the dining halls. In 1973, when I was Master of Dunster House, two black sophomores came to complain that they had been assigned a white roommate. Looking at the records, I saw that one of them had gone to Little Rock Central High School in Arkansas. Before telling the students that they could accept their white roommate or get out of Harvard, I asked the boy from Little Rock High if he saw anything historically ironic in his segregationist attitude. He did not.

Rosovsky resigned from the student-faculty committee as soon as the April 22 vote was cast. He felt betrayed, and he had been. The black students, including the most militant among them, ought to have felt betrayed as well. In the sight of the foolish boy brandishing the meat cleaver and of the student leader who threatened them with harm, the faculty could have taken the opportunity to defend their principles and, more significantly, to tell the students, black and white, that they thought too much of the future of black studies to allow it to go to hell at the hands of incompetents. But instead, they put on their most sympathetic faces and let the mob rule. The vote taken, they could go back to their offices and allow black studies to murder itself. I am not sure the "victorious" students knew what had hit them.

CHAPTER 9

BY THE END OF MAY, the whole place was manic. Every day saw a half dozen meetings of one or another political group, people huddled together in agitated clusters. No meeting came to an end without at least one shouting match. Moments of hysteria were fewer than they had been during the days immediately after the bust, but they still occurred. So many protests and events were held in the Yard that the grass was beaten into a dustbowl. Political slogans such as "Down with Harvard" and "Down with the Committee of Fifteen" were stuck everywhere — on the doors of all the buildings, even on the pillars of Memorial Church. A poster bearing the chant, "Ho Ho Ho Chi Minh, NLF is bound to win!" was pasted to the door of Sever.

In the spare moments permitted them by the fevered political activity, students prepared to take final exams. Teachers prepared to give them. Strange as it was to realize, the spring term of 1969 — whatever else happened —

was going to conclude with the normal event of thousands of students sitting in the dead quiet of vast halls, poring over blue books, balancing equations, and writing orderly essays on Hegel, Schlegel, and Kant.

While all that was going on, and as much as I was caught up in it, I began to feel something happening inside me, like a tune I was writing in my head. Slowly, undramatically, I began to sense a change in my attitude toward Harvard and in my thoughts about my future. It had been a while since I had given any thought at all to my future, since for so many years good things happened to me without my having had to think about them. Yet I had not taken the trouble to ask myself if the sort of success I was having was what I wanted.

Now I began to realize my doubts about university life. Several things had happened or were happening to bring them to the surface. The black studies vote was one. The Morton White incident was another. The reason that White's calling Ford a liar in front of the faculty had such a dispiriting effect on me, as well as on many others, was not only that I saw how quickly and casually the civility of an institution could be tossed aside by those who comprised it; it was also a moment that revealed who many of these faculty members really were. They did not care for the institution, except for what it gave them, and they would not fight for it. Tenure had endowed them with both a freedom to work and a distorting sense of self-interest. They could speak of "community," but they did not really believe in community, and when the chips were down, they showed — by their meanness or by their silence — that they were out for themselves.

Of course, this did not apply to all of them. Kelleher, Handlin, Beer, Baker, Dunlop, Peretz, and Heimert, among others, were as loyal to Harvard as Harvard could hope for. Yet few spoke up. Even Kelleher conceded that he had been a part of a silent majority.

"I remember telling a neighbor when Columbia went bust," he recalled, "that that wouldn't and couldn't happen at Harvard — the faculty would not stand for it. So when it was Harvard's turn I was unprepared and damn disillusioned. From the start, however, I knew where I stood and I always voted my convictions even when I thought the majority I was in was small and fragmented. Yet I never spoke up. Was I sheltering behind the stammerer's privilege — a privilege that normal speakers are unaware of and yet acknowledge? Was I just timid? I don't know. I do know that I am not proud of sitting silent in meeting after meeting, hunched under the descending shower of well-articulated horseshit."

Other discouraging moments, to which I had turned a blind eye, began to come back to me as I started, half-consciously, to build a case for my leaving Harvard. The English department, my department, had a number of honorable souls besides Kelleher, but there were others who made one's flesh crawl. I had been so eager for their favor, I had refused to see them clearly. When I was a graduate student, I would overhear them making fun of my fellow graduate students at department social gatherings, gossiping about and sneering at the drones whom they used as graders in their lecture courses and whom they cowed and terrified.

When my first scholarly article was about to be published in the fall of 1969, Morton Bloomfield, the department chairman, called me into his office. After praising the piece in a perfunctory way, he told me that Harry Levin was gravely upset that I had not cited a relevant work of his in my article. I told Bloomfield that I had not cited the Levin article because I had not read it. "I understand," said Bloomfield. "But Harry feels that you *ought* to have read it, and he would be very angry if you did not mention it." Since my article was to be published in *Harvard English Studies*, Bloomfield was implying, nearly stating, that if I did not cite Levin, my piece might suddenly be disaccepted. Stunned by this intellectual dishonesty, yet swayed by cowardice, I read Levin's article and cited it.

Alice Shapiro, one of the brightest and funniest of my exceptional group of fellow graduate students, referred to the department as "the Great Chain of B-ing." Her pun was based on the coincidence that so many of the department members' names began with the letter "B": Bush, Baker, Bate, Reuben Brower, John Bullitt, Larry Benson. Sitting next to me in class, Alice made a doodle of *veritas*, the Harvard motto, by writing it in English, in the inverted triangular shape of the Harvard shield. In place of the "ve," which is next to the "ri," with the "tas" positioned below, she put "tr" next to "ut" over "h." An old joke went that since the shield appears on Harvard chairs, it allowed everyone to sit with truth at his back.

The department was growing weaker intellectually. Its recent tenure appointments were being given to people who had been favored students and acolytes of the senior people. In terms of imaginative criticism or scholarship, none of the younger appointees — with the exceptions of Heimert and Renaissance scholar Walter Kaiser, who was on leave that spring — could hope to compare with Bush, Kelleher, Alfred, Bate, Baker, Levin, the great poet and translator Robert Fitzgerald, or Daniel Aaron, an eminent scholar of American literature, who was appointed in the early 1970s. There have been several first-rate appointments since — the critic Helen Vendler and the poet Seamus Heaney among them. But of the younger people in 1969, hardly any were original thinkers or inspiring teachers, and this would help to ensure that students would grow less interested in the study of literature and in the humanistic approach to learning.

The dilution of the English department in those years was noteworthy not simply because a few inferior professors replaced a few superior ones, or because the department contained some petty and nasty people. The reason the deterioration of the department — and of the history and philosophy departments as well — was significant at Harvard and other universities at the time was that it represented the deterioration of the humanities everywhere. To be sure, there were several reasons for the parlous state of English studies, including a growing tendency among students to appreciate pictures over words and an exhaustion of material. Definitive scholarship had already been done on the great works from Anglo-Saxon on, and there was little left for criticism to rake over, save contemporary stuff whose worth was yet to be proved. Yet the quality of the people was still the major factor. Looking around at the English faculty under the age of forty-five in the late 1960s, it was hard to believe that this was once the home of Barrett Wendell, Bliss Perry, Francis J. Childe, Robert Hillyer, and the venerable Shakespearean scholar George Lyman Kittredge.

Now the unthinkable happened: Yale's became the most sought-after English department in the country. But Yale — not unlike the radical students everywhere — began taking its subject apart. Thus arose deconstructionism, formalism, Derridaism, and all the other isms that left a humanistic approach to literature in bits and pieces. As Alan Weinblatt, another brilliant graduate-student friend, now an author of critical books on Eliot and Robert Penn Warren, put it, this was "the other Harvard-Yale game," and Yale won.

As the quality of the Harvard English department diminished, the importance and popularity of the social sciences shot up. When I entered Harvard in 1962, English, Comparative Literature, and History and Literature were the concentrations the brightest students were drawn to. Not seven years later, the brightest students were taking economics, social relations, and social studies — concentrations that had less substance but which were taught by smarter and more attractive people who were convinced, and who persuaded their followers, that America's future resided in their classrooms.

But it was not simply the character of the department that was getting to me, it was the entire enterprise of teaching literature. While I had been thinking of teaching as a means to the end of allowing me time to write, I did not take into account the corrosive effect teaching literature has on writing. Universities have become the Medicis for writers since the 1950s, but the bargain rarely works out well for the writers. There is too much self-consciousness about literature. When writers take outside work to support their habit, they are better served by taking jobs that are far removed from writing, so as not to get in the way of it. While writing the "Anecdote of the Jar," Wallace Stevens's day job was vice president of an insurance company. Had he not done work that was antithetical to poetry, he might never have written poetry. Had he been teaching Wallace Stevens, he could not have become Wallace Stevens.

No matter how many students admired certain members of the English department for their scholarship and acuity, they admired no one as much as Robert Lowell, who dropped in from New York once a week for a day or so and taught one term a year. He was angular and bony, with a face full of kindness and madness in equal parts. He gave courses in Shakespeare and in the Bible as well as his poetry-writing seminar. But his attraction lay in the fact that as one of America's great poets, he was the real thing. He made literature, he did not merely make notes and comments on it. When I was taking his poetry-writing seminar, I would go to his office hours in his Eliot House suite, which began early in the morning. Dozens of people showed up — not only Harvard students, but also students from other local universities and people who hung around Cambridge, of whom there were plenty.

In his sun-bright rooms, we would gather, struggling with awe, hope, and intimidation. We would make a great circle around him. We sat on chairs, on the sofa, on his bed, on the floor at his feet. The dust would rise in the streaks of sunlight. Everyone was still. Poems would be presented to him in silence for inspection. He would hold them to the light like a forgery expert, read them aloud, and deliver a judgment.

He was too distant and too private to be called a guru, and he was plainly on the edge. Someone once described him as "Heathcliff played by Boris Karloff." But he was the acknowledged mystical leader of the writers at Harvard, or who came Harvard's way. Lowell had taught poetry-writing at Boston University to Sylvia Plath and Anne Sexton, both of whom had smaller but intense followings of their own. Plath was the better poet of the two, and by the late 1960s a cult had formed around her. Sexton, who lived in the area, gave frequent readings. The day after Plath killed herself in England, Sexton read an awkward and ineffective elegy to her, which she had written that morning in a rush, and which seemed as much an effort to claim Plath's mantle as to express her sorrow.

All these poets had what was called the "confessional" mode in common, but the quality that drew hundreds and hundreds of students to them was their madness. Berryman, too, was mad, which was one of the reasons that that poetry reading in Boylston Hall, where he was "bugged" by Harry Levin, was packed. Of those four, only Lowell did not die by his own hand, and all of them lived in pain and depression, of which they made poems. To the students, they were ideal representatives of a mad time; their poetry consisted of hard lines that were broken up like glass; they saw life as an inner torment; their mythologies arose from their personal psyches. They were the perfect writers for the 1960s and perfect for Harvard, where madness was respectable — for some, perhaps, the goal. The movie *King of Hearts*, about inmates who take over the asylum, ran for the entire decade in a Cambridge theater.

For people like myself, it was Lowell whom one ought to emulate — if it were possible to emulate Lowell and remain sane. But the more one adulterated original writing with literary criticism, the less one felt inclined to write.

After a while, one's authentic language was diluted. Worse: the necessary recklessness that fires good writing is held in check, and soon is tamed. One begins to think of one's work from the perspective of the critic. There is prior restraint. I did not realize it when I was taking Lowell's seminar, but apart from doubting my talent, the reason I was growing less inclined to write poems was that I was paying too much attention to what academic critics might think of them.

Then, too, I was beginning to feel restive as a teacher. I was standing outside not only literature, but experience in general. Harvard undergraduates are prized above all other strata in the University because they are seen as doers, leaders, men and women who are about to be active in the world. Teachers train the doers. I found myself looking upon students like Mark Helprin with a wistful envy, because it was clear that they were bound to plunge straight into life, and I very much wanted to plunge with them. (In the 1996 presidential campaign Helprin showed how ready he was to get near the action by becoming one of Bob Dole's speech writers.)

All the evidence of my feelings had been before me, but until that spring — and undoubtedly spurred by the disruptions of that spring — I had breezily ignored it. Now, like everyone else, I was shaken up. I also knew that I had neither the skills nor the temperament to be a scholar. I studied Irish literature and history by taking long walks with Kelleher along the Charles. In the deep winter cold, we would walk together along one bank, across a bridge, along the other bank, and back to his office in Widener. He would spoon-feed me from his vast bin of knowledge, and I would swallow eagerly. Kelleher was a real scholar, the greatest ever in his field. He had the brains and he had the patience. I am certain that he always knew that I was tagging along for a wonderful ride but that I would drop off eventually.

I wasn't even a very good teacher, no matter what was said in that article in *Newsweek* or by the *Crimson's Confidential Guide* to undergraduate courses, in which English 263 was praised to the skies and called by some students the best they had taken in the college. The truth was, I did not know enough. And I did not care enough, either. I had the bearing of someone worth watching, and I could sense that the students enjoyed following me with their eyes as I talked about books. They even enjoyed the quality I had of being able to teach one thing and appear — by a distant stare — to be thinking about something else. Often I *was* thinking of something else. But what the brighter students honor in their favorite teachers is the quality of worry. They like to see teachers worry about the material, and they like to overhear them worry. That, I think, is what the best teaching is — being overheard as one worries aloud about a subject. That was not me. I learned just enough to raise the essential problems, and my mind was just inventive enough to come up with one or two new ones, but I lost no sleep over whether a jar was or was not important to Tennessee — the question was merely an intellectual riddle to me — and I think my more scrutinizing students knew that.

I also realized I did not like the students as much as I had pretended to. I had affection for individuals, of course, but there were certain general assumptions evidencing themselves in that particular segment of baby boomers which were alien to me, and to my generation. They were governed almost entirely by sympathy for individual causes. The politically active students were sympathetic with the Vietnamese. They were sympathetic with the American underclass and with American minorities. They were sympathetic with women, with the American worker. Later they would be sympathetic with homosexuals. Everything they did that spring was out of sympathy for one or another "victim."

All that was fine as far as it went, but that was as far as it went. The impulse to tear down traditional structures to exert a sympathetic reaction was not followed up by the creation of new and improved structures. Long after 1969, Michael Walzer wrote to me: "Was I right, am I right, in thinking that student anti-war politics in 1969 was a bad sort of politics? But maybe, in the short run, the children of the elite had to act badly in order to convince their parents that the war could not, should not, be continued? Had those same children acted as I thought they should, formed organizations, and inter-University correspondence committees, and argued at meetings, and published pamphlets, and marched in disciplined, peaceful demonstrations — would it have had the same effect? The cunning of history requires craziness and passionate intensity . . . and quietly rational social democrats only afterwards to clean up the mess . . . can that be right? I don't think that I believe it. Better to have acted then in a way that could have been sustained and that other people, different sorts of people, could have joined."

When Tony Lukas wrote his article for the *New York Times Magazine,* he expressed admiration for the students, their causes, and their tactics. Today, he told me: "I have the advantage of hindsight. When I look back, I can see that what the students were doing wasn't a movement that had much philosophical grounding, in terms of what lasted. The kids were driven by an anxiety about the draft. They wanted to be heroes outside a war, so they made a battlefield in Harvard Square. But I'm disappointed that the New Left didn't have more legs."

Looking back, Rappaport said: "I regret the extreme militancy with which radical politics were practiced, because it did alienate an important social movement. It certainly contributed to the fragmentation of the Democratic party."

It was not only what the New Left was not doing; what it was accomplishing was to embolden right-wing America. Even Michael Kazin, looking back at the twentieth anniversary of the Harvard Strike, noted the harm his generation had done by encouraging the emergence of conservative forces. And he told me that he now thought how naive they all had been about forging a worker-student alliance. "Still," he said, "we helped stop a very bad war."

After a typically ludicrous faculty meeting, Ernest May, a historian of American diplomacy, stopped Jim Wilson in the Yard. "On this campus," he said, "the men of conscience outnumber the men of honor." In the spring of 1969, Harvard was but one of the places where the influence of sympathy began to look like Gargantua — a sweet baby monster.

And the more radical students were so irritatingly cocksure of themselves. From one point of view, they had reason. As Kazin said, they helped bring the Vietnam war to an end. Student protests such as those at Berkeley, Columbia, and Harvard had an enormous effect in amassing public opinion against the war. Television, too, was a powerful antiwar influence; and, as Michael Arlen's brilliant *New Yorker* pieces on television's news pictures of the war explained at the time, images of the costly, wasteful, ill-inspired venture brought nightly into the nation's homes exposed the war for what it was. But had those pictures not been accompanied by the student marches, the student boycotts, the moratoriums, and the ferocity of acts against staid and establishment monuments like Harvard, which acts provided the sound and fury that went with the television pictures, who knows how long Vietnam might have seemed a sound idea to U.S. presidents? Anyone who watched worn-out Lyndon Johnson announce that he would not seek re-election in 1968 knew that he had been brought down, to a large degree, by children.

That said, one cannot give the protesting youth as much credit as they give themselves. The Vietcong, too, had something to do with ending the Vietnam war.

And there were several less admirable effects of their so-called victory. Respect for the military life, which had been high in the country through the early 1960s, plummeted. One way the students at Harvard showed their guilt about their privilege and safety was to scorn those who went to Vietnam, and when the war was over, to shun them. Al Gore, who volunteered for Vietnam after his graduation in 1969, recalled the time in the following September when he returned to Cambridge on leave. "My hair was cut short," he said, "and I wore my uniform. I walked through the streets of Cambridge, and I became so angry at the presumption of those who instantly shouted epithets and sneered."

The more long-lasting effect was on foreign policy. For good and ill, the generation that came of age in the late 1960s has resisted going to war on any and every front. Galbraith said to me: "The people in opposition to Vietnam gradually came into positions of influence, and now we have a much more strongly resistant attitude to take military action outside the borders of the United States —

much stronger. That is undoubtedly a residue from that earlier experience. What we were willing to do in Vietnam, we were extremely reluctant to do in Somalia or Haiti."

So great is that reluctance that no discrimination seems to be made in deciding whether to intervene in Panama, Haiti, Somalia, or Bosnia. "People [of my generation] just took it for granted that they would have some kind of secure future," Jim Fallows observed. "That accounted for the ease of the dismantling of institutions. It was not only Vietnam that affected the more isolationist foreign policy of recent years; there is still a reflexive peacenikism." It derived from the assumption that if the institution of the government was for intervention in genocidal Bosnia or genocidal Sudan, intervention must be wrong. Of course, if the government itself were in the hands of certain baby boomers, it might not be for intervention, either.

The student radicals had a reflexive contempt for the liberalism that was my generation's creed. Their contempt persists today. It takes forms ranging from political correctness (conservatism in liberal clothing) to prissy attempts at censorship and a neopuritanism that would be laughable if anyone had the wit to laugh at it. On bookstore shelves are titles like *Raising Self-Reliant Children in a Self-Indulgent World* and *Getting Your Kids to Say "No" in the Nineties When You Said "Yes" in the Sixties.* There is a strong movement to put moral education in public schools, and moralists like William J. Bennett (*The Book of Virtues*), whom parents in the late 1960s would have laughed out of town, and whose book is filled with absurd interpretations and misinformation, they now take seriously. These developments may, in fact, do some good in a vague, atmospheric way — indeed, they have done some good — but the single-minded, righteous ardor with which they are pursued reminds one of the political pieties of not that long ago. The belief that this generation knows the right and true path has not changed very much and still represents their assault on liberal tolerances.

In 1971, Archie Cox was shouted down when he attempted to speak at a "Teach-In" on Indo-China in Sanders Theatre that was sponsored by the conservative student organizations Young Americans for Freedom and the Harvard Young Republicans. What he tried to say, over the shouts of student protesters who drowned him out, was that he felt that "the impetus for reform and renewal in the United States during the next few decades must come from the student dissidents." He added, however, that "in many respects their energies are misdirected, their thinking is simplistic, and their tactics are both self-demeaning and self-defeating. They have not yet learned the whole spirit of liberty: neither the knowledge that liberty is not the ruthless, unbridled will; nor [have they learned] the humility that seeks to understand the minds and failings of other men; nor the spirit that is not too sure that it is right."

Finally, so many of this emerging generation were ridiculously self-conscious. They continually analyzed and

ROGER ROSENBLATT

congratulated themselves. They blithely dismissed their parents' generation, which had not only won an undeniably good war, but had also initiated civil rights movements without which the boomers' individual rights movements could never have gotten off the ground. The civil rights movement began in the late 1950s when the Harvard class of 1969 were eight and nine years old.

The radical students around me acted as if they had invented social awareness. Yet it was the generation that came out of the Second World War — the people who saw the Nazi death camps — who first confronted the social ills of the late twentieth-century world. In 1945, James Thurber collected *The Thurber Carnival*, including the moral fable of "The Rabbits Who Caused All the Trouble," a tale of the Germans and the Jews. Billy Wilder produced *The Lost Weekend*, which in a way was the first antidrug movie, the drug being alcohol. Rodgers and Hammerstein created the brooding musical *Carousel*. All that was in 1945. And between that year and Korea in 1950, America was given *Gentleman's Agreement*, an indictment (if a tame one) of anti-Semitism; Robert Penn Warren's *All the King's Men*, an indictment of demagoguery; *Death of a Salesman, Summer and Smoke*, and *A Streetcar Named Desire* — indictments of conformity and repression.

The students were not only sure they were right; they were sure they were wonderful. Peter Kramer (class of 1970) wrote an unintentionally hilarious piece for the 1969 commencement issue of the *Crimson* that could have succeeded as a parody (though not at the time), called "I Am Frightened (Yellow)," an echo of the off-color Swedish film *I Am Curious (Yellow)*. "No one can pretend to have a clear vision of what happened," wrote Kramer, "if he fails to realize that the brightest and most creative people at Harvard were in University Hall."

Nicholas Gagarin wrote the following account of University Hall in the *Alumni Bulletin:* "What was most euphoric was us and what we were to each other . . . we were very beautiful in University Hall, we were very human, and we were very together."

So earnest was this belief that individualism was a self-justifying virtue that some people never outgrew it. In a special issue of the *Crimson* (April 22, 1994) commemorating the twenty-fifth anniversary of the takeover and the strike, Richard Hyland (class of 1970), who was one of the occupiers of University Hall, offered a personal testimony. He told the *Crimson:* "I don't think the protest should be judged by whether or not it was successful in getting ROTC off campus, ending the war in Vietnam or whether the regime in Vietnam was good or bad. What was in our power was the changing of ourselves. If we were successful at that, then what we produce . . . is what we should be judged on." Hyland is a professor of law at Rutgers.

For all those reasons — and because of my innate failing to sustain interest in any place or enterprise for very long — I began to drift away from Harvard. Whenever I could, I spent time with Carl. He was always an anxious child, being the first, very good, kindhearted, astoundingly alert, and painfully conscientious. It was hard on him, that spring, with his new sister getting so much attention and University madness keeping me away from home most of the day. Lost in my own thoughts, I wasn't as attentive to him as I ought to have been even when we were alone together. In the late afternoon, when time permitted, we would sit on the living-room rug and listen to the Beatles sing "Rocky Raccoon."

If a weekend gave us a free day, Ginny and I would take the children on drives into New England. We would call ahead to a real-estate agent in some picturesque New Hampshire or Vermont town and pretend that we were in the market for a house. I am sure that the agents saw through us, but they dutifully showed us around. It was not a house I was looking for, it was a place other than Harvard, and every "farmhouse with barn and pond and acreage in field" that we admired was not a potential weekend retreat, but a new home and a different life.

"Where do you see yourself in five years?" Ginny would ask me on the drives home.

"I don't know," I told her.

"Teaching?"

"I suppose," I said without conviction.

"I don't think so," she said. "I don't think we'll be at Harvard or at any university in five years."

"How do you feel about that?" I asked her.

"I don't know," she said. We drove in silence through the New Hampshire hills, which were purple and on the edge of blossoming into the brief, bright New England spring.

Most often I took my confused thoughts on long, meandering walks around Cambridge, and as the spring wore on, I hoped that they would lead me to a new direction. One morning I wandered into a law class taught by Alan Dershowitz on the rules of evidence and was mesmerized by his brilliance at argument and in making the pursuit of justice fun. As a journalist, I have ridiculed Dershowitz for his egotistical extravagances, but he was a fabulous teacher.

I would go over to the graduate center on Ash Street and play the piano in an empty sitting room. I would loiter around the kiosk at Harvard Square. The subway, or Metropolitan Transit Authority (MTA), whose unnavigable interconnections were made famously funny in a folk song popularized by the Kingston Trio in the 1950s ("Oh, he'll never return, no he'll never return"), was under construction or repair in the Square for all eleven years that I was at Harvard. One day I asked a workman: "Are you fellas ever going to finish this job?" He told me: "Jeez, I *hope* not, mister."

I would take my long walks down to the boathouse, up to Brattle Street, across to our old neighborhood of Wendell and Oxford, through the little attractive streets of brownstones and frame houses, like Trowbridge and Ware, and then down toward the river again. Cambridge away from Harvard was so quiet during the day, as compared to the Square and the Yard. A teakettle shrieked in an old frame house. A soprano sang scales.

I thought of a discussion I had had with Kelleher as we walked along the river. I had reread "The Second Coming" and was wondering about Yeats's phrase "mere anarchy." Why *mere?* Kelleher suggested that Yeats was using the word in the old sense of "sheer" or "utter." But I asked him if mere might mean casual, easily and carelessly created. He nodded, allowing that my interpretation might be a possibility. Now, looking around me, I wondered if anarchy were not always mere — people turning on one another as if on a whim and casually bringing down their own house on their heads.

I realized that I no longer felt like an innocent. As soon as I began to question why I was at Harvard, I sensed the sudden presence of sadness in my life. I knew only what I did not want. It may have appeared differently to anyone who bothered to observe me, but I knew that I would never be the fair-haired boy again, that the world of gifts and blessings was no longer mine. I was treading a path that, no matter how beautiful and inviting it looked originally, would lead me to places of darkness and unhappiness. I followed it, nonetheless, because I had nowhere else to go.

CHAPTER 10

A T DINNER in the House on June 7, which was the night before the Committee of Fifteen met to decide on discipline, an SDS student stood at the end of the cafeteria line, apparently waiting for me.

"Everybody thinks that you're going to save our necks," he said in a low growl, "but I think you're going to sell us out."

"What would selling you out mean?" I asked him.

"Expulsion," he said.

"Don't you want to be expelled?" I asked. "Think what it would do for your martyrdom."

"Fuck you," he said. "I always knew you were against us. All that sweet talk about the rightness of our cause, how you hated the war, blah blah blah. That was all bullshit, wasn't it?"

We were holding up the rest of the line, so I swung my tray around him and headed for a table. He followed close behind me, murmuring the word *bullshit* louder and louder. I sat down and he remained standing.

"I am against the war," I said. "And I am on the side of people protesting the war."

"But you'll go ahead and throw us out of college, won't you?" he said.

I was exhausted and would have preferred to stand and shove my tray of food down his throat. But instead I told him calmly that I could not say how I was going to vote.

"You're going to make a lot of enemies," he said. I turned away from him and began making innocuous conversation with the students at the table. They seemed unnerved by this confrontation. I knew that they were frightened of this kid, who had already shown that he would not hesitate to use his fists.

"Bullshit," he said again.

"How're you guys doing?" I asked the table.

"Bullshit," again. He was reddening as I ignored him. It was gratifying to have seven or eight years on a boy like that. We could have passed for the same age, but I had long overcome that fierce, sputtering awkwardness of adolescence, and I also knew how to needle him.

"Bullshit," he said, as I chatted amiably with the others, pausing only to ask them: "Does anybody hear bullshit?"

Everyone laughed. I could feel the SDS student grow rigid with anger behind me. He was not bright or quick-witted, but he was committed. I would not have been surprised to feel a chair come crashing down on my head. But he yelled to the group: "You think he's on your side, but he's full of shit! You'll see!" As he stomped out of the dining hall, I asked: "Please pass the salt."

While it took no special gifts to appear superior to my attacker, I knew that he was right. I was a bullshitter to those radical students, and perhaps the worst kind of bullshitter. I had never said that I would vote against expelling the students involved in the takeover. They had assumed, from my prior Ad Board rescue efforts in their behalf, from my antiwar stance, and from my I'm-always-on-your-side personality, that the idea of throwing students out of college for the takeover of a building would be horrifying to me. Indeed, a year earlier, it might have been. But, though I never developed anything approaching a keen definition of my politics, a year or two of watching fanatics at their sport had greatly reduced my admiration for them, no matter how much I believed in at least some of their causes.

Since I had been at best vaguely radical, I was growing just as vaguely conservative. I was a bullshitter to my students because I had never come out and said that I deplored what they had done, and were continuing to do, to the University. I never indicated that I would be pleased to see the more violent among them thrown out. I could always hide behind the excuse that the workings of the Committee of Fifteen were to be held secret and that, in any case, the members were supposed to keep open minds until all those "findings of fact" were in. The truth was that from the moment I had learned that deans were hauled out of their offices and shoved downstairs, I knew I wanted those kids punished — even if I did not know that I knew it at the time.

There was an argument for feeling this way that could have appealed to me from the days of the civil-rights protests. To break the law in the name of some higher morality is to assume that one will pay a penalty. If you want to change an unjust law, keep breaking it, in as public a way as possible, until the lawmakers capitulate or are won to your side. Sam Beer rose at the Paine Hall faculty meeting to tell his colleagues that they would do the students "no favor" by being lenient. He meant of course that punishment is an integral part of civil disobedience.

But the feeling that had been growing in me was not nearly so sophisticated. It went back to that belief in the sanctity of certain institutions — especially the university, any university, which, when I was seeing clearly, I treasured as the one place in American society where the country's defining freedoms were not only protected, but also nurtured and celebrated. I was, deep down and in secret, Gerschenkron and Bloch. When I reached into the caves of this belief, I was even in favor of maintaining the presence of ROTC on campus — not to give ROTC academic standing, but to allow it to remain as an option for anyone seeking the military life or needing it to complete an education. What Jim Watson had said to the faculty about ROTC being useless was nonsense to me. In a worthwhile war, who would not wish to be led by a more thoughtful and educated first lieutenant?

I would never say such a thing, however, and that was the trouble with me. I knew that I could have my opinion two ways, or three, or four, keep it to myself, and mislead those who might believe that I would be for them no matter what. I could rationalize my deception by claiming that I *was* for them, that by wanting violent actions condemned by the University I was on their side in more permanent ways than a momentary leniency would indicate. But in truth I was just playing it safe, for as long as I could, in the interests of being loved. I thought that being loved was the most important thing in life, and though I was older and more sophisticated than the students, that is where I proved how young I still was. In any event, I was about to lose playing it safe as an option.

The committee members were tense and tired when we met the following day, on June 8. Wilson looked grim. He undoubtedly feared that what he called the "mush-head thinking" of the faculty, which had prevailed in the black studies vote, would prevail here, too. The students, Keith MacAdam, Renée Chotiner, Bob Blumenthal, John Read, and John Fernandez, looked edgy for opposite reasons. They could sense from the discussions of people like Hoffmann, Heimert, and myself, who were identified as liberals, and from the quieter members of the committee like

Ben Schwartz, John Edsall, and Don Anderson that there was little hope for letting everyone off with a warning, or in official terms, a "suspended suspension." Read told me recently that there was "a high degree of consensus among the students that the right course was to discipline for violent acts." But my memory is that their idea of discipline fell short of expulsion.

Dunlop, too, looked anxious. He might have entered into the committee's work hoping that all the students identified in the University Hall occupation would be bounced, but he was too sharp not to see what disruption that would cause. It was not a verdict that the majority of the committee would have permitted. The whole idea of determining different levels of culpability was to enable the committee to mete out different levels of response.

He and Wilson may also have made a tactical error. They professed to want to discipline those who cursed out the deans during the takeover as severely as those who pushed them around. According to Read, this "bad-language issue" caused the students on the committee to caucus at Keith MacAdam's apartment in an effort to reach a consensus. Of course, knowing Dunlop, he might have pretended to want to expel the foul-mouthed protesters in order to have an extreme position to retreat from in a negotiation.

As uncomfortable as it had been for the faculty members on the committee to function in the community during those weeks, the student members were the ones who had to deal with their fellow students, including many who were in University Hall, on a day-to-day basis. Throughout they seemed remarkably composed for their young ages. "The process we devised to hear complaints and methodically work through the cases was very important to the results we achieved, in my view," said Read. "The patterns of behavior emerged more clearly, and it bought us all (including Wilson and Dunlop, I guess) time to deal more objectively with the facts."

The petition that had been delivered to the committee and signed by over two thousand students made it clear how most of the young people felt: No one should be expelled, and the protesters — while they may have acted badly — were in the right. The petition consisted of six short paragraphs, the first of which was typed in block letters: "WE STAND BEHIND THE PRINCIPLE THAT NO ONE SHOULD BE SEVERED OR SUSPENDED FROM HARVARD DUE TO THEIR ACTIONS AT UNIVERSITY HALL." It went on to say that "although many of us question the use of disruptive tactics, we believe that those students who participated in the occupation . . . acted from strong moral and political convictions. That the issues raised were significant and legitimate is demonstrated by the subsequent actions of the faculty."

In other words, many petitioners might question violent tactics, but the tactics had worked. The faculty had voted to get rid of ROTC and to establish a department of Afro-American Studies. The petition also noted that students who had been arrested were already subject to punishment by the Cambridge court and had a police record. The kicker was that "expulsion from the University will place the men involved in serious jeopardy of being drafted."

This last argument hit home with many faculty members. The draft situation had already altered academic standards at universities throughout the country. For a period of time, students whose grade averages fell below C were eligible for the draft, thus every college in the country was suddenly grading as inflatedly as Harvard. Long before University Hall the Ad Board had been aware of the jeopardy an expelled student faced and had acted with special leniency, even for that body.

In short, the petition, unlike most fliers and broadsides published that spring, was not a hysterical document. It stated soberly that suspension or expulsion would "only be divisive and appear vindictive." And it was carefully conceived. In declaring that no student should be thrown out, it included "those presently on probation," because the petitioners knew that in disciplinary matters three strikes, or even two strikes, and you're out was a standard practice. The committee had to take such a petition seriously, and the student members of the committee, perhaps most seriously.

On the other side of the issue was the nature of the event. As united as was most of Harvard in the opinion that the bust was wrong, Pusey's decision had no effect on how one felt about the original occupation. That, not the bust, was the act on which the Committee of Fifteen was assigned to make a judgment. If the committee had wanted to, it would have been possible to lump the takeover with the bust, and with the validity of the SDS demands, and with the moral rightness of the antiwar movement itself. But the committee's decision to divide its task into thirds made that blurring impossible; it had to go ahead and focus on University Hall for what it was, or appeared to be, and thus exclude the wider, potentially mitigating factors from consideration.

When the committee sat down to weigh the evidence at hand, all the events subsequent to the University Hall takeover evaporated, and we were left with an unclouded picture of the precipitating incident. Up to the point that Deans Glimp, Epps, and Watson testified before the committee, all that had happened in University Hall had been known by way of the newspapers or the rumor mill. Now the committee had the transcribed testimonies of the principals. These were sanitized, often stilted, and much dryer accounts than the ones that were published, but they were curiously more dramatic and affecting. The testimonies were accompanied by a map of the interior of University Hall, clearly showing Areas A, B, and C — which designated the north, south, and middle of the building — and which assigned numbers to the halls, doors, and staircases that had heretofore existed in our imaginations as a kind of dreamwork maze. The clarity of this piece of paper, too, had a definite effect on the committee.

"At approximately 11:50 A.M. on Wednesday, April 9, 1969," Archie Epps stated, "I was at a meeting in Dean Glimp's office on the first floor of University Hall. While in Dean Glimp's office I heard students coming into Area B. I then went outside Dean Glimp's office to Area C and saw about ten persons already in the area. I then went up staircase B and passed about six persons on the first flight of stairs. Some people were saying, 'Get Epps out of here.' Some other people were following me up the stairs. I could hear a tambourine in the background. I proceeded up the second flight of stairs which was quite crowded. Many persons were shouting at me, 'Get him.' Others said, 'Don't let him get in that room,' apparently meaning the Faculty Room. I was then surrounded by five or six people and pushed down both flights of stairs into Area B where there were approximately 20 persons standing watching. I was then pushed out door #4.

"Soon thereafter I re-entered the building through door #3. There were a great many persons on staircase A. Others were streaming in door #1. There were approximately 30 persons milling around in Area A. Some persons started shouting at me that I was responsible for killing people in Vietnam and shouting obscenities at me. People were moving all around me very quickly and there was a lot of shouting going on. I was then pushed out door #6.

There was a huge crowd of at least 500 people standing in the Yard on that corner of the building."

Fred Glimp's testimony also began at the entrance of the occupiers. He, too, noted the sound of the tambourine. He told his secretary to leave the building, went to the Faculty Room, and saw that a large table had been placed across a door and that about a dozen students were inside. He then went to Ford's office to report on what was happening. He continued: "On leaving Dean Ford's office, I encountered a student in the anteroom and requested that he leave at once. He replied in substance that this was not my office and I had no authority to ask him to leave. At this time, Bill Toby, the University photographer, had stepped into the doorway between the corridor and Dean Ford's waiting room and took a picture of the student with whom I was speaking. The student promptly seized Toby by the arm, and said he was going to make a citizen's arrest, and refused to release Toby until the photographer had identified himself.

"I then went down staircase A into Area A. There were probably about 25 students in Area A at this time. I attempted to return through door #7 but was prevented from doing so by two students standing in the doorway, one of whom had his arm across the door, his hand holding the door frame. I then went up staircase A again to Dean Ford's office. I informed Dean Ford that administration officials were not being allowed to go into their offices. There were about four students in Dean Ford's anteroom at this time, and these students informed us that we were expected to leave. Deans Ford, Elder and myself then went down stairway A. Dean Ford told an assembled group of about 25 persons standing in Area A that they were interfering with the work of University Hall and he instructed them to leave. This warning was met with a jeering and shouting response.

"Deans Ford, Elder and myself were then told to leave the building at once. Dean Ford asked if he could at least get his coat. After some discussion, the three of us went back upstairs to Dean Ford's office for this purpose. There were students on each of the landings on staircase A. On one of the landings, Dean Ford asked the students whether they wanted to discuss anything, to which he received a negative response. Dean Ford then said to the students, 'If it is clear you are evicting us, we will walk out.' Deans Ford and Elder then preceded me down staircase A and I stopped to talk with a group of students standing on the first landing. In the course of this discussion, a student began yelling at me: 'You better get the hell out of here.' While standing on staircase A, I also noticed an undergraduate who had attempted to enter the building and who was expressing views against the takeover of the Hall. This student was held by two others while a third punched him.

"I was then physically but with undue force ushered into Area C, through Area B and out to the building through door 2."

Bob Watson's testimony began in a similar way to the others'. After instructing his secretary to leave, "I then went out into Area B towards the Housing Office which is on the northeast corner of the building. People were bursting in the northeast door, some of whom were going up staircase B and others were pouring into Area C. There was considerable noise and excited talking amongst those who were entering the building.

"I went up staircase B passing groups of persons on each landing. At the top of staircase B, I was grabbed by one student but was let go soon thereafter at the instruction of the persons present. People were still coming up the stairs in large numbers. As I came out of my office into Area C, I was grabbed by one person but I pushed him away. At this time I also saw Dean Glimp being barred from Area C. More and more physical force was being used to evict personnel at this time. I was grabbed from behind on both arms and pushed into Area A. There was a great deal of noise and confusion in Area A at this time. I was then pushed out door #4 with such force that I was knocked into three or four people. These steps, however, were jammed with people thus preventing me from falling further down the stairs."

The effectiveness of these testimonies lay in their flat precision, dead language, and lack of color. Nothing was embellished. None of the obscenities was quoted. No personal feelings of fear or anger were recounted. As a result, these plain, absurdly formal documents took on a dignity of their own, as well as the sobering power of fact.

The issue came down to numbers. If no one of the 135 identified was expelled, if probation was the most severe punishment meted out, the message would be that assault and battery were deemed worth only a slap on the wrist. If a great many were expelled wholesale, it would set off a riot and in any case would not be fair. Everyone on the committee understood this peril of extremes, even if the student body did not. I think it was Milton Katz who had originally proposed the hearings to discover which occupiers did what exactly, and in so doing, he saved the day. Of course, it is possible that had the accused students testified they might have refuted the deans, but I doubt it. The more violent protesters boasted elsewhere that their acts were justifiable in the larger context of their beliefs. Unless one thought that the deans were lying about who shoved whom, the basic facts of the incident were not in contention. And thanks to Katz, the committee was able to focus on the facts. What might have appeared in the beginning to be simply a normally sound judicial procedure turned out to be the best way to try to come to a reasonable decision.

The fact-finding had produced a few names of those who had pushed the deans around, another somewhat larger number who had touched the deans, another number who had chained the doors, and the largest number who had been present at the occupation but had not used physical force. How now to proceed? How to vote?

This was a highly unusual moment for me; I actually knew what to do to achieve the ends I realized I desired. From my experience on the Ad Board, I had learned that if there were a number of students proposed for different gradations of disciplinary action, the way to ensure that no blanket punishment occurred, which would normally be the more severe punishment, was to take up the more serious offenders first and then work down. The logic went that if one wanted to keep the punishments less severe overall the best tactic was to struggle for something less than the most severe punishment possible for the worst offenders. Once that category had been established and filled, it was easy to proceed to lesser and lesser levels, and to reserve the least severe punishment for the largest number of offenders. If, on the other hand, one started with the least culpable and established a fairly severe punishment for them, it was inevitable that the most culpable would get the book thrown at them.

Accordingly, once the levels of participation were determined, and the names of students were slotted into each category, I proposed that we start from the top. Seeing what I was doing, Wilson and Dunlop opposed my motion. But I made up some gibberish about having had experience with these types of decision-making mechanisms on the Ad Board, and argued, in the most grandiloquent terms, that top-to-bottom produced "the fair results which I know we all seek."

Wilson and Dunlop were not buying, but they knew that I did not need to beat them by the force of my argument. Most of the committee members had arrived at the meeting intent on keeping the more severe punishments to a minimum, and it was fairly easy to draw dividing lines among the levels of participation in the takeover. We made our decisions from the top down.

In the end, of the 135 students identified as being in the building, sixteen were asked to leave the University. Of these, six were seniors and would not receive their degree at commencement, which was four days away. The most severe punishment was given three students who had manhandled the deans — who had grabbed them, hustled them out of their offices, or shoved them down the stairs. These three were "dismissed," which meant that they were only able to be readmitted by a two-thirds vote of the faculty. Five others who used less force on the deans or who chained the doors or damaged property were "separated" for one year or two years. Six others were "required to withdraw" for one year or for one term. No student was expelled permanently or expunged.

Of the remaining group, ten were placed on probation, and the great majority who did no physical harm were "admonished" for being involved in the occupation.

I found these decisions to be exactly right, and I am sure — from the votes that the committee took —

that most of the other faculty members did as well. Our student members may have felt that the dismissals were too harsh — Renée Chotiner and John Fernandez seemed especially glum — but by tossing out a few of the more culpable, a necessary line had been drawn between violent and nonviolent protest.

The committee could not make these decisions on its own; it had to recommend them to the faculty, and so the rest of the afternoon was spent in determining how best to make our presentation. The faculty meeting was scheduled to be held the next day, June 9, in the Loeb Drama Center. First, Heimert would present the order of the business at hand. Hoffmann would give the report of the history sub-committee. Anderson would give an "interim progress report," which was to say no report, on governance. Now it was time to choose those committee members who would make the most-anticipated report.

It was agreed that Dunlop would speak on the rationales for the various levels of discipline and that Wilson would spell out the findings and the specific actions taken against individuals. To protect their privacy, the names of those who were disciplined were never published by the committee. The individuals involved received letters informing them of their status, and if they wished to make them public, that was their privilege. Some chose to do so. But to this day, the University has not made the names known. The minutes of the June 9 faculty meeting would not include the findings of fact and the names that Wilson reported.

There was one matter of business left: to choose the committee member who would present the Resolution on Rights and Responsibilities to the faculty. The resolution had to be offered up for a vote, and the vote had to be positive, because if there were no formal agreement reached on common rights and responsibilities, the whole idea of discipline could be tossed out the window. If one did not agree on rules of behavior, one could not agree on what constituted misbehavior, and logically there could be no punishment.

I knew from one quick glance at Dunlop's intently innocent face that he had maneuvered to have me make that presentation. He had, without my knowledge, gone around to every member of the committee to persuade them that only I could be entrusted with this delicate and indispensable assignment. Why me? Because I was Mr. Everything-to-Everybody, and I was still too young to have made the sorts of faculty enemies who would shoot down what I proposed simply because I had proposed it. Above all, I was so terribly presentable.

When Dunlop asked, "Roger, will you do it?" I knew the fix was in. Yet scared as I was at the thought of getting up and addressing that body, I was also excited. I knew what Dunlop knew as well — that by playing point man to the subcommittee on discipline's presentation, I was putting myself in the middle of the subcommittee's decision to expel the sixteen students. I was in it now, for all the Liberal Caucus and all the students to see. No longer could I, by a sympathetic glance or a sympathetic smile, connote that coward's ambiguity by which I had, to that moment, lived. "Roger, will you do it?" meant, "Roger, are you ready to act like a grown-up?"

"Sure, John," I told him.

CHAPTER 11

THE SHOES were too tight, but I bought them anyway. My old shoes looked like they had barely survived a shredder, so I told Ginny that I simply had to buy a new pair. How could I appear before the Harvard Faculty of Arts and Sciences in such ratty-looking shoes? And what shirt should I wear? And what tie? And was my suit okay? I mean, what difference did it make? I couldn't go out and buy a new suit then and there. It ought to be a suit and not a sports jacket, right? I should buy a new pair of shoes, right?

Ginny yessed and noed at the appropriate intervals in an effort to calm me down. I had spent the morning of June 9 writing my introductory remarks to the Resolution on Rights and Responsibilities. Now it was noon, and the biggest problem in the world was my shoes.

We went to a shoe store on the ground floor of Holyoke Center, and I tried on a pair of the kind of shoes I had never worn in my life. They were fancy brown loaferlike shoes with leather tassels where the laces would have been on normal shoes. They were too pointy for my feet, and they pinched my toes.

"What do you think?" I asked Ginny.

"Won't it bother you that they're tight?" she asked.

"They're fine," I asserted. We left the shop, I stiff as the Frankenstein monster and limping. It was now close to one o'clock. The faculty meeting was set for two. We went back to Dunster House, where I dressed, rehearsed, redressed, and changed my shirt, which was soaked with sweat.

I limped up to the Loeb Center. Wilson and Dunlop saw how pale I looked and signaled me to sit between them. The theater was packed, of course. University police were stationed in the halls; that had never happened before. A preliminary motion was passed to permit WHRB, the Harvard radio station, to broadcast the meeting, and to allow two *Crimson* reporters to attend, until the disciplinary proceedings were called for. Then the reporters would be asked to leave. Pusey called the meeting to order at 2:10 P.M.

There were a few preliminaries. Ford rose to assure the faculty that the late date of this meeting was not the product of a conspiracy to make the Committee of Fifteen's decisions known only after a great many of the students had gone home. By June 9, mostly seniors remained on campus, commencement being scheduled for June 12. He said that the absent students would all be sent a mailing containing the votes and the discussions of the meeting about to occur. He added: "We can't prevent some students from coming back in the fall and being greeted with a shower of innuendo on this score, but it seemed well to have the great majority of them given the chance to study the actual documents over the summer, and know what did happen, before they return to start arguing about it."

Peretz asked Pusey to tell the faculty what response the University was making to the subpoenas coming from congressional committees.

The Dean of Admissions, Chase Peterson, who later became president of the University of Utah, responded that the College had not sent the Senate committee the names of any students involved in the University Hall incident. To the request that Harvard provide the names of students receiving government scholarship aid, the College responded that the names were already available through the Office of Education, and if the Senate committee wanted them, it could obtain them that way. The committee chose not to, Peterson said.

Hilary Putnam rose and asked if, given the actions of Judge Viola, Harvard had been "sincere" in stating that it would argue for criminal charges against the occupiers to be dropped.

Pusey, always ready to shoot Putnam down, told him that his question was "not related to the question about the subpoenas." Archie Cox then answered Putnam, saying, in effect, that Harvard had given its best effort to have the charges dropped, but had failed.

Thomas Cottle, an assistant professor of social relations, asked Pusey if a buildup of police protection was planned for commencement. Pusey told him to address the question to the University Marshal. Peretz rose again to ask why University Police were present in the Loeb Center. Pusey responded that it was "a precautionary measure."

By the time Heimert stood to announce the main order of events, everyone was on edge, no one more than I. Hoffmann gave his "Interim Report on the Causes of the Present Crisis." It condemned incidents like University Hall, and it condemned the University for helping to create such incidents by paying too little attention to the student outcries. Hoffmann said: "There is a need to defend this institution against violence . . . because the kind of progress which many of us hope for is possible only if, to begin with, the University is saved. But the kind of progress we have in mind is one which could be summed up in one word: an opening — an opening of our minds, which need a restoration of trust among the various parts of this University, and opening as a method, as a way of involving more people at all levels."

The report, which was followed by supporting statements by Ben Schwartz and Bob Blumenthal, was deliberately vague, and had any of the angrier faculty members wanted to punch holes in it, they could easily have done so. But no one was interested in that report or in the one that followed on governance, presented by Don Anderson, which was really the promise of a report to come at some time in the future. The moment now arrived that people *were* interested in. The faculty secretary announced: "Professor Rosenblatt will be presenting the Report on Rights and Responsibilities."

I was trembling as I started toward the lectern, yet the nearer I came to it, the calmer I felt. This was a wholly new experience for me. I had never spoken at a faculty meeting before. I had never before addressed a large audience in a potentially explosive situation. Yet, for some reason, when I stood at the lectern and looked out over all those tense and straining faces, I felt not only in control but serene as well. There they were, all whom I admired and despised, looking to the youngest among them — for what? I held them still with my eyes. I could have stood there forever. I learned at that moment the odd fact that I am at my most comfortable in a social circumstance when speaking before hundreds or thousands of people, perhaps because it is most like being alone.

On page one of the *New York Times* the following day was the story about the faculty meeting and the decisions reached by the Committee of Fifteen. On the jump, where the story continued, was a picture of me — the only picture with the story. I looked like a contemplative schoolboy wearing a jacket and tie. The caption identified me as Briggs-Copeland Instructor in English, a member of the Committee of Fifteen, and a member of the Liberal Caucus, thus covering practically all my bases. The article stated that I had presented the resolution, and quoted it in full in a box, along with my introductory remarks.

When I began to speak, my voice reverberated pleasantly in the theater. I tried to release the tension in the room by a combination of slightly unusual language and a little wit.

I called the resolution "a curiously unimaginative document" in that it was only a reminder of "principles that ought to be self-evident." I said that it "represented the efforts of many men who do not necessarily hold the same convictions but who can and do agree on the essential properties of a great university." I then waited a beat and added: "Unfortunately, Mr. President, the unification of ideas does not always cooperate with unity of style. No fewer than seven writers produced this resolution. You have before you, sir, one of the most extraordinarily stylistic exercises that has ever assaulted this faculty." The remark was more academically cute than funny, but, given the circumstances, it broke the place up.

Then I read the resolution. It said that a person who enters a university "neither surrenders his rights nor escapes his fundamental responsibilities as a citizen, but acquires additional rights as well as responsibilities to the whole University community." The rights included the expression and advocacy of opinions, and the pressing for those opinions, but did not include "violence against any member or guest of the University community, or deliberate interference with academic freedom and freedom of speech, or the destruction of property."

There followed a paragraph stating specifically the levels of action to be taken against anyone engaging in the violation of the above rights. It was this statement that set up the presentation of the disciplinary actions to follow, and the faculty knew it.

In a preemptive move I then noted that some people might ask why we needed so detailed a document, and I said that without specificity we were unprepared to deal with violations of rights. I conjectured that some people might also think the resolution not specific enough, and I countered that no enumeration of violations could be exhaustive. Finally, I said, there were those who might ask why we needed such a document at all. I responded: "Mr. President, any community that depends on printed guidelines for its survival is doomed to destruction in its own clauses and subclauses. . . . It is to say that the success of this statement will not ultimately be measured by its adoption in this room, but by its adoption in the conscience of the University." This last observation was quoted in the *Times*. I sat down, and now I was trembling again.

There followed statements of support and challenges by the faculty. Sam Huntington, a leader in the Conservative Caucus, commended the committee's work but asked for a clarification on the matter of harassment. I rose to reply that harassment was included as one of the violations of free movement and free speech. John Cooper, professor of government, rose to ask if faculty members were also subject to discipline. Holton answered that this was still an interim document and that the question would be considered. Michael Walzer, in his role as leader of the Liberal Caucus, reiterated that the document needed the widest discussions and consultations to be fully accepted, and that it required the strongest commitment on everyone's part to agree on common principles. Hilary Putnam rose to ask the defeat of the resolution on the grounds that the University was complicit in the Vietnam war, and in genocide.

That both Huntington and Walzer spoke in favor of the document practically guaranteed its passage. I was certain that Dunlop had been at work, negotiating a deal. He had been. Equal numbers of Liberal and Conservative Caucus members supported the resolution, each expressing enough reservations to placate the more fanatic members of his constituency. Finally, a vote was taken. The resolution was passed by 365 in favor, 21 opposed.

In a sense, the presentation of the specific disciplinary action that followed was anticlimactic. Dunlop and Wilson were well prepared, clear, and forceful, and while there was some opposition to the committee's decisions, the motion passed by 342 to 29. It had taken two months to the day, but at last the takeover of University Hall had come full circle. The meeting adjourned at 6 P.M.

There remained one more event for the Committee of Fifteen, which was scheduled for an hour later, at 7, in Memorial Church. Before the faculty meeting had begun, Hoffmann had suggested that all the members of the committee make themselves available to the students and anyone else who might be interested, to answer questions about our decisions at a public meeting. I barely had time to get home. Ginny asked how things had gone, and I told her that our motions had passed by large pluralities, but that I could not really tell how things had gone. I had seen no student reaction. I had seen no students. The Dunster courtyard was eerily empty, as were the streets. I passed very few people as I walked up to the Yard, and in the soft gold light of dusk, I almost felt at peace.

When I entered the Yard, however, and began to cross the quadrangle, I saw hundreds of students and others swarmed around the entrance of the church. Arriving at close to seven o'clock, I made my way through the crowd, which became one long, menacing murmur. I entered the church and saw that all the pews were filled, packed tight, and I realized that the huge crowd outside represented those who could not get in.

On a stage that had been set up for the occasion sat several of the committee members facing the audience. I joined them in the second row, beside Hoffmann. We sat in two rows, with Milton Katz seated dead center in the first. Though this open meeting had been at Hoffmann's urging, it was Katz who took the hot seat. He, who had advised the committee on legal procedures and had chaired most of our meetings, now took it upon himself to explain the committee's decisions rationally in what I assume he thought would be a civilized public forum, with various points of view expressed, and questions and answers.

By ten minutes after seven, the entire committee was seated, staring forward at the packed pews of the church, and waiting for Milton to begin. The church was steaming hot, due both to the weather and to the number of bodies inside. Milton turned to his left and right and behind him, where I was sitting, to ask if we should get started. Nervously, we nodded, and he began to speak. In that excessively precise voice of his, which seemed anything but comic on that evening, he told the crowd that the committee was available to answer any of their questions.

Things started in a fairly orderly way, with individuals standing in their places and challenging the committee to justify its actions. The first few questions, which were more like short speeches, were very angry but were presented in such a way as to allow responses from the stage. Milton attempted to give answers, but the crowd made it impossible for him to complete his thoughts by jeering at practically everything he said. He persisted, nonetheless. When he invited another committee member to attempt a response, that person would get the same treatment. Dunlop or Heimert would try to get out a whole sentence but would be drowned out by hoots and boos. Wilson, the crowd would not allow to speak at all.

Soon the volume rose to a level that overwhelmed everything anyone on the stage was saying. We were the enemy, and it made no difference what we would say. It became apparent that the crowd were not there to listen or to argue, or even to prove us wrong. They were there to punish us. First one member of the audience would rise and shout something at us. Then, before anyone on the stage said anything in response, another person would shout something else, and then a third, and then five or six at once.

The noise was louder than any crowd at a ball game or an antiwar rally. It had a different pitch, more like a scream than a shout, and it was so sharp at the edges that the meaning of the phrase "cut the air" came clear to me. When one thought it might abate, it was merely mounting a second wind, and it returned twice as loud as it had been. In no time, the din of the voices was going on its own. It required nothing of the people on stage to inflame it but our presence. By 7:30 the church itself became the noise, a roar in which slogans, clichés, long tirades, and epithets massed together. At one point, a speaker shouted something about "hysterical women" and was immediately swallowed up in shrieks of "chauvinist pig" and shrill laughter. I watched the back of Milton's head — small, white, motionless. None of us could move. I did not think that the crowd would storm the stage or do us harm. They had actually moved beyond that. They had created one vast howling pandemonium, which engulfed the church for at least twenty minutes and was fed by itself.

Hoffmann, who was seated to my right, leaned forward and said to me, in a remark made funnier by his French accent, "You know? I've had better ideas."

CHAPTER 12

THEY SAY that it never rains on the day of a
Harvard commencement, and even when it does,
nobody remembers it the following year, so the
adage remains intact. No pretense was necessary on June
12, 1969. The sun warmed the Yard, the name of which
became the Tercentenary Theatre for the occasion. The
days before had been busy with preparations. Long
chains of folding chairs were set up facing Mem Church
and filling the Yard from the church to Widener and
from University Hall to Sever Hall. A deep stage was
erected directly in front of the church. There the governor of Massachusetts, the mayors of Boston and Cambridge, judges, and other state dignitaries would join
the Harvard Corporation, Overseers, faculty, and administration. We would all sit together in our mortarboards
and hot, bright robes and hoods and face the graduating seniors and their family members who had come
to watch another class of Harvard undergraduates be

welcomed into "the fellowship of educated men and women."

Nearly four thousand students would receive degrees, including members of all the graduate schools. The undergraduates numbered 1,115, of whom 70 percent would graduate with honors. An SDS protest was planned for the ceremonies, which was described by the *Crimson* as "an expression of general dissatisfaction with the College and in support of their eight SDS demands." Protesters planned to wear red armbands and would walk out in the middle of the ceremonies, carrying placards and chanting. The sixteen students whom the Committee of Fifteen had dismissed or suspended issued a statement denouncing their punishments but said that they would make no appeal or take any retaliatory actions. The committee's decisions, they said, were "consciously political" and "part of a nationwide conspiracy to smash SDS." They would not conduct a special protest at commencement.

I was up and robed by 7:30. Ginny would have the children dressed and ready for the afternoon degree-awarding ceremonies in the Dunster courtyard. In spite of the armbands, which seemed to be worn by most of the students, and the slight anxiety caused by the announced protests, the mood of the day was that of every commencement — robust and full of cheer and pageantry. Pappenheimer lent me his red Harvard doctorate robe. I walked out of the Senior Tutor's residence, joked with a few seniors who were standing around with their parents, then headed for the Yard to take my place in the procession.

At 8:45 there were chapel services for the seniors. At 9:15 Governor Francis W. Sargent of Massachusetts arrived from the State House to stand beside Nate Pusey and prepare to proceed to the stage. He was accompanied by the National Lancers of Massachusetts, wearing scarlet coats.

Then the seniors, in caps and gowns and armbands, gathered in the Old Yard. Alumni and other dignitaries of the day, including the honorary degree recipients — Mayor John V. Lindsay of New York, David Rockefeller, former secretary of the interior Stewart Udall, president of the United Auto Workers Walter Reuther, and the poet Marianne Moore — gathered in another cluster and prepared to be led to the stage by the High Sheriff of Middlesex County, who carried a large, ornate scepter, which he pumped up and down in the air in front of him. At a signal from the University Marshal, all swarmed into the Yard, the seniors preceded by the Harvard band making a great, brassy noise.

Was it finally over? Had the most disruptive and wrenching time in the University's modern history petered out to this? Hardly. Commencement was merely a moment's quiet, a brief bow to tradition. What had occurred in the prior two months was never going to be over.

Harvard's upheaval was not simply a typical war of the late 1960s between the radical students and University officials. It was a deeper and more far-reaching conflict between older and younger sensibilities, between those who believed in institutions and those who wanted to tear them down, between those who were driven by sympathy for individual causes and those who stood with traditional social structures. The eruption in Mem Church was the howl of the baby boom about to come into its own. What began with a single explosive incident in the Yard exposed an entire generational rift and touched upon antagonisms that have not been mended to this day. For the country as a whole, "fuck authority" would become "fuck" business contracts, institutional loyalties, a broad liberal arts education, the liberal tradition itself, the ideal of the melting pot, even human contact. It would become — in the words of that desperate boy in the Yard — "Fuck everybody."

Within the University, so embittering were the events of those two spring months that when nearly thirty years later I contacted the people who were there to ask their opinions of what the events meant, their passions seemed as alive as they were originally. Oscar Handlin wrote to me: "I am still not able to distance myself from [those events] adequately. Some years ago, I thought of writing a brief account which would be candidly partisan. But in the end I gave up the idea. The passage of time did not lessen the impact of the tragedy; indeed, the unfolding consequences since 1969 have cast a lurid light on the tragic disaster of that year."

Tommy Lee Jones told me: "I have trouble writing about it. It is too personal, and far too difficult to be concise." Archie Cox said that "the events at Harvard . . . were too important to my life to attempt a casual answer to your question."

Bill Alfred spoke to me of his amazement at how quickly the University disintegrated. "The thing was smashed," he said, "the common trust between students and faculty, smashed. It never healed."

Kelleher said, "The University has never recovered from the damage that was not only inflicted, but was institutionalized then. There is no likelihood that I will ever feel kindly towards those who, as I believed then and still believe, betrayed the vocation and laws of scholarship for the luxury of identifying themselves with righteous causes — the luxury, in other words, of self-conscious moral rectitude."

Pusey wrote me: "The late 1960s were a sorry time. I compared the attacks made on the universities in the early 1950s, the McCarthy era, from the outside, with those made by students and faculty from the inside in the 1960s. In my view then and now, there was little justification for, or merit in, either set of attacks, unless the present prevalence of locked doors and ensuing bitter faculty squabbles are to be judged such."

Jim Wilson, who left Harvard for UCLA in the late 1970s, sent me a note that read: "I am happy to report to you that I have successfully repressed all recollections of the spring of 1969. My last memory of the sixties was of the Red Sox playing in the World Series of 1967; my next recollection is of George McGovern losing to Richard Nixon in 1972. In between, all is lost. Ah, merciful oblivion."

In some cases the feelings were still so raw that a few people directly involved in the events would not respond to me at all. They may not have wished to dredge up a painful time or to reexamine their involvement in it. Or they may not have trusted me to report their participation fairly or give what they would consider just weight to their points of view, since I, too, was directly involved and eventually adopted a position that, as far as I could tell, was mistrusted by everyone.

In any case, it soon became clear that what had occurred in those two months was devastating to the University. Of all with whom I spoke about it decades later only Stanley Hoffmann thought that little lasting damage had been done. Everyone else recalled a disaster.

The odd thing is that none of the destruction would have occurred had there not emerged a strange conspiracy between those who wanted power and those who readily ceded it to them. The fact that student radicals wanted to take over Harvard, or all of America, for that matter, did not condemn them. However naive much of their revolution was, for the majority of them it was sincere. Even most of those who for personal reasons protested Vietnam to avoid fighting there were sincere in their objective opposition.

Yet they never could have created so much chaos at Harvard had the administration and most of the faculty not allowed them to. The administration cooperated with the people who wanted to take the place apart merely by overreacting and behaving stupidly. But the faculty's role was subtler and more morally careless. There were certain critical moments in those two months when professors had the opportunity to instruct their students usefully merely by voting the right vote or by saying the right things — things in which they supposedly believed. Yet, for the most part, they offered no opposition to what they disagreed with, as if to tell the students: "If you want it, take it." Liberalism rolled over on its back like a turtle awaiting the end. I do not know why, but there was an impulse running under the events of that spring to let things go to hell, and it was acted upon by young and old alike.

As for me, I too came apart after that spring. As the commencement began, I took my place in one of the front rows on the far left side of the stage and looked out at thousands of people fidgeting and murmuring with excitement. The families of the graduating seniors were dressed up, colorful as flowers. Small children, bored by the long ceremony, ran in and out of the rows of folding chairs.

I stole a glance at Marianne Moore, who was sitting to my right, wearing her black dress and trademark tricorner hat. She looked small and serene, like a bird. I had seen her once before, when she had visited Jack Sweeney's English 263. She had read the class the poem "The Mind Is an Enchanting Thing," and in the middle of her reading, as if to demonstrate the poem's thesis, she stopped. "I don't like this line," she said, of a poem that had been anthologized in stone for decades. And she changed it on the spot.

The mind is "not a Herod's oath," she had written in that poem, that "cannot change." Sitting on the stage, waiting for the ceremonies to begin, my mind was changing. I, who had dug myself a hole so deep in Harvard, and who was about to dig deeper still, felt suddenly transported from the place, as if hooked by a giant crane and hoisted up high over Cambridge and far away. I had turned Harvard off that spring, like a spigot. My life to that point had been spent in anticipation of a career in a university. Now, though four years were still ahead of me at Harvard, I intuitively knew that I would be leaving that place and that life forever.

What I could not foresee was how my exit would occur, and how much I would have to do with it. After the spring of 1969, I was no longer a hero to the students. I remained a popular teacher for a while, but the radical students especially saw me as a traitor who had sold out to the Committee of Fifteen. SDS pamphlets attacked me. In the Dunster House dining hall, there was no longer the approving warmth that had greeted me before. By voting to expel students, I had declared myself to be one of "them," the Harvard administration and the conservative faculty. I was not one of "them," but I was not one of the students either, anymore. The Liberal Caucus grew suspicious of me, as

I had less to do with them as well. And I did not feel like explaining myself to anybody, out of a combination of pride, arrogance, and a growing desire to live on my own terms. I did not know it in the beginning, but I was headed for a solitary existence, which often made enemies simply by being, and which was to characterize much of the rest of my life.

Yet all that was very slow in coming, and by the fall of 1969 and for a year or two afterward, I was still riding on the fumes of my former popularity. My star as a teacher was rising. The English department, learning of the success of my informal black literature course in Dunster House, asked if I would teach it for credit in the fall. I had no doubt that they were motivated by political expediency. But I was happy to comply. The course was listed as a conference group, which was meant to accommodate about twenty students. The first day of class in September, four hundred students showed up, and Black Fiction in America immediately became a popular lecture course.

I was also offered a contract by Harvard University Press to write a book on black fiction and was given a $1,500 advance — a fortune for a university press book in those years. I was awarded a Canaday fellowship of $2,000 by the Faculty of Arts and Sciences. Harvard put me up for a Younger Humanist Award given by the National Endowment for the Humanities, for the nation's most promising teachers. I won.

My reputation continued to rise among my faculty peers and with administrators, or it appeared to do so. A faculty council was created in the fall of 1969 to represent the faculty and make major decisions in concert with the administration — this as a product of its distrust of the administration. I was elected overwhelmingly. I was made head of a Committee of Rights and Responsibilities, which was charged with writing a final version of a Declaration of Rights and Responsibilities as a sort of moral contract to be applied to any future disruptions. I wrote the declaration. I continued to run freshman English. The position of University Ombudsman was created to settle or head off future disputes. I was the man. When Papp decided to step down as Master of Dunster House in the spring of 1970, John Dunlop, who had succeeded Franklin Ford as Dean of the Faculty, asked me to take the post, which previously had been occupied only by permanent faculty members. At twenty-nine I became the youngest House Master in Harvard's history.

That summer of 1970, the Harvard Corporation began the process of selecting Pusey's successor as president. The Corporation published the first of a series of diminishing lists of the names of those whom it was considering for president. The first list had some two hundred and fifty names on it, and I was pleased, though not entirely surprised, to be on it.

Ginny and I rented a summer house in Truro, on Cape Cod, where I began work on the black fiction book. We looked ahead to our suddenly aggrandized lives in the Master's Residence of Dunster House. The residence was a small mansion connected to the east wing of the House, consisting of eleven bedrooms, huge public rooms, and secret closets.

The lists of potential Harvard presidents were published at intervals throughout that summer and into the fall. Two hundred and fifty became one hundred became sixty-nine became twenty-three. My name stayed aboard. By the middle of the fall, I could feel the growing suspicion and dislike of my colleagues — junior colleagues especially. Marty Peretz told me: "We looked at you and said, 'Why is *he* getting all this?' On the Liberal Caucus we called you a turncoat and thought that you were now in the camp of Wilson and Dunlop." He then added something that would not have been true of him, but would likely have been true of some others: "I also think that we were jealous."

When a *Newsweek* article on the final twenty-three appeared showing my picture along with that of Dunlop, Michigan State president Clifford R. Wharton, and Derek Bok, the popular dean of the law school, the hatred and the dark gossip were growing thick.

Ginny and I spent our nights in our new, cavernous home at first talking only about the subject and then avoiding it. The setting of our conversations was like a scene out of *Citizen Kane* at Xanadu. At one point, after the list of sixty-nine came out, before it got down to the final twenty-three, and the rumor started to rise that, in fact, I might be the anointed, I considered writing a note to the Corporation, saying thanks for the honor, but that I was wholly unqualified and unprepared to be Harvard's president. I could have added that I did not want to be Harvard's president as well, but that would have seemed superfluous. I decided not to write the note because I assumed that my name had been on those diminishing lists for cosmetic reasons (*Newsweek* had noted that being Jewish and twenty-nine, my chances were less than slim). I thought I had been given a pat on the back for having turned out to be a responsible citizen on the Committee of Fifteen, and I believed, therefore, that when they got down to the finalists, my name would be gone. I decided not to withdraw, in other words, because I did not want the selection committee to think that I had the gall to presume that I had been a serious candidate in the first place. By the time the final list was published it was too late to do anything but sit and stew.

One evening, Ginny and I were invited to a dinner for about ten people at the home of law school Dean Derek Bok and his wife, Sissela, the philosopher, with whom we were becoming close friends. Upon entering, one of the guests saw Derek and me standing together and blurted out: "Well! What's this? Candidates' night?" I gulped and did not smile. Derek saw my embarrassment and immediately diverted the conversation. It was the sort of act of kindness toward a young man that was but one of the many gifts that qualified him for the Harvard presidency. When at last the Corporation chose him, no one was more pleased, or grateful, than I.

The weird thing is that in those days the Corporation actually might have selected me. Several faculty members said they were betting on me, and the reason was that in an atmosphere in which every reasonable decision was overturned, every civility abandoned, every tradition made expendable, and in which no one trusted anyone else, anything, especially the ridiculous, could happen. A Christmas poem in the *Globe* contained the couplet:

> *For Harvard's departing Nate Pusey a cheer*
> *And unnamed successor (of thirty) we hear.*

Youth was given undue prominence and exalted respect merely because it was youth. After the Harvard selection process, I was approached by a half-dozen colleges and universities inviting me to be considered for their presidencies and was presented with one offer outright. I am certain that most of the places knew nothing about me but my age.

By the middle of the 1970–71 academic year, I had arrived at an oddly unhappy point. I was trying to get out of Harvard at the same time that Harvard was trying to get rid of me. Their effort was made easier by the fact that in a year I would be coming up for tenure, and I had given the English department nothing to indicate that I was worthy of tenure. The fact was that though I had been a good teacher for a while, I was not deserving of tenure. Students sometimes clamor to have tenure given teachers who do no research, but tenure probably ought to be reserved for people who can teach well and add some original, interesting research to a discipline.

Not only was I not producing any research, the quality of my teaching was also going down. Within two years the Black Fiction in America course that had started out with such high-minded enthusiasm was drawing less than half the original number of students — not only because the political cachet was wearing thin, but because I was not giving it any spirit. I was killing it by means of laziness and dullness, as I was also killing my once-treasured Modern British and American Poetry course. I ran freshmen English with less than my left hand. I gave no effort to the Faculty Council, to which I was reelected once, and then not elected. In short, I was creating the circumstances by which others would rightly find me wanting and so in effect was shooting myself by hiring a hit man.

I was making decisions that I knew would irritate my enemies and confuse my friends, but I made them anyway. We bought a Mercedes — a used one, but a Mercedes — an affront to the academic world of VW Beetles, especially when made by a junior faculty member. The car was white. We also finally bought that farmhouse in New Hampshire — a dilapidated wreck with rolling floors and a dry cistern. We bought it because we loved it and because we wanted a place to call home away from Cambridge, but the idea of a junior faculty member buying a country home before he was awarded a permanent position appeared to others to be an act of pure audacity. The Boks let us use their Belmont house for the academic year 1971–72, when I took a leave of absence, and our friendship with the new first family of Harvard infuriated those who would be infuriated. I was not suitably humble, and I made no move to indicate that I thought it proper to be suitably humble.

Things came to a head when, during my year's leave, the English department requested that I present material by which I would be judged for tenure. At first I thought not to present anything and to state that I did not want to be considered — not that I believed I had a chance in hell. But Ginny persuaded me to go through the motions as an act of respect for Kelleher, Sweeney, Alfred, Baker, and a few other senior members who had encouraged me as a student, and who, Ginny argued, would be insulted by my turning away now. I did not know that Ginny was right (neither did she), but I went ahead and dutifully submitted my stuff, in part because I wanted that suicide-by-murder, and perhaps, too, because I was still reacting like the good competitive boy, who, while not wanting the prize he was seeking, also did not want to have it denied.

Yet I also managed to ensure that the department would turn me down, in case there was the slightest chance that they would not do it on their own. Over that summer in Truro, I had produced about four-fifths of the black fiction book, a manuscript of over two hundred pages, which, had I presented it to the department, might have at least made them pause before canning me. (The book was eventually published by Harvard University Press in 1974, was a considerable critical success, and still sells a few copies every year.) I did not submit those pages to the department; instead I gave them a very brief introduction to the book and nothing else. Later, long after the department had made its decision, Jack Bate took me to the Faculty Club for a drink and lamented: "You should have produced a book."

One morning in the fall of 1972, when we had returned to Dunster House from our year off, Alan Heimert, then the department chairman, came to the Master's Residence to give me the bad news. Alan and I had forged a sometimes tense but genuine friendship in the wars of 1969. I regretted the thought of not being with him anymore. As we sat together in the sunny dead quiet of the overfurnished Master's Residence living room, I felt his regret as well. Strangely, I felt regret about leaving the University, too; the end of a long time had come. Harry Levin offered to get me a permanent lectureship, a sort of lower-class tenure appointment, which he undoubtedly could have swung. But I did not want to give people the idea that I was willing to hang around Harvard on any terms, and more to the point, I knew that was no longer my life.

When Heimert left that morning, I sat alone staring at a gilt-framed portrait of a Harvard notable over the sofa and thought about my future. One reason I had let my star sink so easily was the same reason I had let it rise; I believed that life was meant to come to me, and not me to it. Now, the time had come to outgrow that nonsense and to decide what I wanted to do with the years ahead. If I really wanted to write, then write. The riots of 1969 had taught me that I was not quite the careless charmer I had supposed myself to be and that I believed in a few things after all. I was beginning to know myself. In the summer of 1973, Ginny, the children, and I would load up the car, and after eleven years, I would drive away from Harvard, having received an education.

All of that lay ahead of me as I sat on the stage of the June 12, 1969, commencement. The ceremonies were over by noon. The SDS students held their walkout. Officials frowned, but not much was disrupted. Everyone headed back to the Houses, where the degrees were to be presented to each senior individually. A small platform had been set up in a corner of the Dunster Courtyard with folding chairs out front for the seniors' families and friends. Papp gave a short, sweet speech. I followed with a short, unfelt speech. I wished the students well. They gave me a standing ovation, but many did not mean it.

After that, punch was served from a huge glass bowl, and the graduates stood and chatted with their families in the bright sunshine. Ginny and I moved easily among them. We said our good-byes. By late afternoon the courtyard was cleared. Students piled into their family cars and were off toward home. Alumni, the same. Ginny and I changed into jeans and took the children for a walk.

Ahead for Harvard were years of more strife and protests through the early 1970s, to be followed by the quiescent 1980s and this content and anxious decade. The University, like most others, would build up an increasingly larger bureaucracy to deal with the problems of which the 1960s made it aware. It appointed its first-ever University counsel in Daniel Steiner, an exceptionally able and thoughtful administrator, to handle burgeoning legal problems in a frequently litigious atmosphere.

Bok turned out to be a great president — a combination of a strong mind, a strong back, and a sure but not adamant sense of right. When there was a student takeover of Massachusetts Hall in the early 1970s over University investments in South Africa he did not call in the police, and the protest fizzled. As with corporations years later, there would be more emphasis in the University on management and less on adventurous leadership. But there also would be more concern for courses in ethics, for a fair distribution of minority students, and for other issues that had to do with equality. The corrupting excesses of political correctness, segregated bilingualism, nationalism, and multiculturalism, which also lay ahead, could not obscure the real advances that had been made. But they could make those advances taste bittersweet at best.

Ahead for the country were Kent State and the Christmas bombing of Cambodia and Watergate and all the sadness, wildness, and disintegrations that characterized the era. One could not see into the details of the country's future, but one could sense how nerve-racking things were going to be. I never felt the same after that spring, and it was not because of anything that I had brought about or that had happened to me. I did not feel that I belonged in my time, or that I knew my country anymore. There had been a great eruption in the earth, and the grass and rocks were upturned everywhere. No matter how smoothly the land might be restored, one knew what it was like underneath, and one's stomach churned.

I wheeled Amy's carriage out the Dunster House gate. Carl drove his rattling red fire engine recklessly on ahead. Ginny took my arm. We walked along Memorial Drive, on which cars rushed by packed with students going home. They shouted to one another from the car windows, and waved and cried, and sped into America.

INDEX

229

INDEX

INDEX

INDEX